I0005982

A History of the State Paper Office

You are holding a reproduction of an original work that is in the public domain in the United States of America, and possibly other countries.You may freely copy and distribute this work as no entity (individual or corporate) has a copyright on the body of the work.This book may contain prior copyright references, and library stamps (as most of these works were scanned from library copies).These have been scanned and retained as part of the historical artifact.

This book may have occasional imperfections such as missing or blurred pages, poor pictures, errant marks, etc. that were either part of the original artifact, or were introduced by the scanning process. We believe this work is culturally important, and despite the imperfections, have elected to bring it back into print as part of our continuing commitment to the preservation of printed works worldwide. We appreciate your understanding of the imperfections in the preservation process, and hope you enjoy this valuable book.

A HISTORY

OF THE

State Paper Office;

WITH

A VIEW OF THE DOCUMENTS
THEREIN DEPOSITED.

By F. S. THOMAS,

SECRETARY OF THE PUBLIC RECORD OFFICE.

" Unsunned Treasures lie in the State Paper Office."—I. D'ISRAELI.

LONDON:

JOHN PETHERAM, 94, HIGH HOLBORN.

MDCCCXLIX.

CONTENTS.

THE History of the STATE PAPER OFFICE, here presented in an amended form, was first included in a Work intituled "Notes of Materials for the History of Public Departments," privately printed by the Author. The tokens of approbation with which the production has been favoured have encouraged him to submit this part to the Public, with additions, uniformly with his History of the Exchequer and Treasury*, both being portions of the Design which he has contemplated, of furnishing information respecting Public Departments and their Records and Documents.

Rolls House, January 1849.

---

* "The Ancient Exchequer of England; the Treasury; and Origin of the present Management of the Exchequer and Treasury of Ireland." London, 1848.

THE STATE PAPER OFFICE.

As the documents in the State Paper Office do not commence generally until the time of King Henry the Eighth (although a small number of instruments of earlier date are found to have been deposited there), a few observations relating to antecedent periods seem to be necessary before commencing the immediate history of the department, for the purpose of guiding the inquirer to the repositories where the earlier documents are to be sought.

Under the Anglo-Norman Dynasty the affairs of State in England were managed by the King's Council, in which the Chancellor officiated, and where he exercised such of the functions of a Secretary of State as those early times demanded, and he had an office to prepare the Public Instruments, in the nature of a Public Office, and not at first a Court of Justice; to him was entrusted the supervision of all Letters, Charters, and other Public Documents which required to be authenticated, and the most formal and solemn manner of authenticating State Documents was by the King's Seal, which the Chancellor had had the custody of, probably from the earliest times of Seals being used. The organization of Chancery rapidly expanded, and in respect of State Documents we find that it became the duty of the Prothonotary of Chancery to write, pass under the Great Seal, and enrol Commissions, Treaties, Leagues, Ratifications, and other Instruments which passed between the Sovereign of this country and other Sovereigns and States; also Commissions, Powers, and Orders to Ambassadors, Patents to Consuls, Diplomas, Declarations, and Grants of Honor and Additions of Coats of Arms to all persons being Foreigners, Pardons of Outlawry, &c.

Like legal proceedings the early State Documents were enrolled, and are preserved in Chancery, both domestic and foreign; the latter come down to 22 Jac. I., when the Prothonotary of Chancery ceased to enrol the instruments made out by him, and his functions gradually ceased, or such as remained fell into other hands. There are also remaining amongst the records of the Chancery many documents from which the enrolments were made, as well as correspondence which was not enrolled; a Calendar of the latter is printed in the several Reports of the Deputy Keeper of the Public Records, viz. Fourth Rep. App. II. pp. 140–164.; Fifth Rep. App. II. pp. 60–96.; Sixth Rep. App. II. pp. 88–115.; Seventh Rep. App. II. pp. 239–276.; and in the Eighth Rep. App. II. pp. 180–184. A Calendar and notices of many documents which were found on the files in Chancery have also been printed in the Reports of the Deputy Keeper.

In process of time the business of the State began to be executed in a less formal manner, and to be diverted into other channels, and the King's Secretary (who was at first styled the King's Clerk, then Secretary, afterwards Principal Secretary, and who probably about the time of Queen Elizabeth was first called Secretary of State,) gradually was employed to execute much of the business formerly pertaining to the Council. But long after the office of Secretary grew into importance, many matters, letters, petitions, &c., were still addressed to the King, to the Council, to the Chancellor, Master of Requests, &c., which afterwards it became the duty of the Secretary of State to receive. This however is not the place to discuss when the establishment and various alterations in the different Public Departments took place, it is sufficient to observe that the King's Principal Secretary had become in the time of King Henry the Eighth a personage of so great importance that his rank and precedence was determined by Stat. 31 Hen. VIII. c. 10., and the business and correspondence of his office so much increased as to require in the same reign a second Principal Secretary, and subsequently a third. Each of these Secretaries, prior to the establishment of an office for the reception of their papers, as distinct from those of Chancery, had the custody of the papers accumulated in his department.

At length in the year 1578 an office was established for the reception of State Papers, and Dr. Thomas Wilson (then Master of Requests, and afterwards one of the Secretaries of State) was appointed Keeper and Registrar of the Papers concerning matters of State and Council, It was not however until the time of King James the First that these papers were reduced to the form of a library, having before been kept in chests.

A Patent of James I. dated 15th March 1609–10, after setting forth the importance of preserving and well ordering Papers and Records, especially such as concern matters of State and Council, as well respecting Negotiations with Foreign Princes as other instructions and directions, recites,—

" The careful endeavours of Robert Earl of Salisbury, our
" Principal Secretary and our High Treasurer of England,
" to reduce all such papers, as well those that heretofore
" remained in the custody of Sir Thomas Lake, Knight,
" being the papers of some of the Principal Secretaries of
" our Predecessors, as also some such papers as he shall
" think fit to depart with, being either such as he hath
" collected of his own times, or such as were left to him
" from his late father the Lord Burleigh, then Lord High
" Treasurer of England, into a set form or library, in some
" convenient place within our palace of Whitehall, to be
" at all times the readier for our use, and for the use
" of any of our Principal Secretaries hereafter, for the
" better enabling them to do us service :"

And then appoints Levinus Muncke one of the Clerks of the Signet, and Thomas Wilson, Keepers and Registrars of the Papers and Records so to be collected and preserved.

On the death of the Lord Treasurer Salisbury in 1612, as stated in the first volume of State Papers, published under the authority of the Commissioners for printing and publishing State Papers, the King's commands were given to his successor Thomas Earl of Suffolk, the Lord Privy Seal, Edward Earl of Worcester, and Sir Julius Cæsar,

Chancellor and Under Treasurer of the Exchequer, to take possession of the late Lord Treasurer's papers and deliver them to Muncke and Wilson. The subsequent Patents especially mention the office to contain the papers of Robert Earl of Salisbury. At this period the papers which had been hitherto kept in chests were reduced into the form of a library as before stated, and the King assigned certain apartments in his Palace of Whitehall for their reception. And the part of the palace finally appropriated to this purpose was the Tower over the gateway which connected the eastern and western parts of the edifice, standing across the street now known by the name of Whitehall. The apartments consisted of two rooms, three closets, and three turrets, of all which entire possession was not obtained until 1618. Although the papers escaped the fire which consumed a great part of the palace on 12th January 1619, yet they were thrown into great disorder by having been hastily cast into blankets.

Great losses of State Papers are said to have taken place during the time of the Rebellion, temp. Car. I. A large portion of the documents, however, relative to the affairs of the Commonwealth are regularly entered, and safely preserved in the office.

We find from a Report of a Committee of the House of Lords, made on 19th January 1705–6, the neglected state of this Office, and what documents had not been delivered. In consequence of that Report an Address was presented to Her Majesty to direct some proper method to be taken for the future to preserve the Papers of State for the use of the public. And with reference to this subject, the following observations occur in the Preface to the before-mentioned first volume of State Papers:

" The office was found in a great state of neglect when
" visited in 1705 by a Committee of the House of Lords.
" In consequence of a Report from that Committee an
" Address was presented to the Queen, in which it was
" stated that, with the exception of the papers of three
" Secretaries of State, viz. Sir Edward Nicholas (restored
" to the Secretaryship after the Restoration), the Earl of
" Arlington, and Sir Joseph Williamson, and those left by

" Sir Leoline Jenkins, few papers had been delivered into
" the office since the year 1670, and those not perfect. The
" address recommended the repair and enlargement of the
" office, and that the papers should be sorted and digested,
" and bound in volumes. After a reference to Sir Chris-
" topher Wren, it was determined that the upper floor of
" the Lord Chamberlain's lodgings at the Cockpit should
" be fitted up and appropriated to the State Paper Office.
" This was accordingly done, and an apartment of eighty
" feet long and twenty-five feet wide, which is known by
" the name of the Middle Treasury Gallery, was then added
" to the office.

" In this state it remained until the old gateway was
" pulled down, about 1750, when the contents were found
" to have greatly suffered from vermin and wet. The papers
" contained in the gallery which was left standing remained
" there, but the contents of the rest of the office were
" removed to an old house in Scotland Yard, where they
" remained, and suffered still further injury from wet, till
" 1819, when it became necessary to pull down the last-
" named house; and the papers were again removed to
" another old house in Great George Street, the corner of
" Duke Street, in which, and in the Treasury Gallery, they
" remained until 1833, when they were removed into the
" present office in St. James's Park, built expressly for their
" reception.

" In 1764 a Commission was issued for arranging,
" indexing, &c. the papers, and continued until 1800, when
" the above Commission was revoked, and a small establish-
" ment of clerks was allowed to the Keeper of State
" Papers."

On the 10th of June 1825 a Commission was issued for
printing and publishing the documents of the State Paper
Office (which has been renewed to the present time, the
Commission of the 2d of July 1842 empowering the
Commissioners to print Calendars also), it having been
then considered, as stated in the Commission, that the
documents were in a great measure arranged and indexed.
This statement, however, would seem to be rather premature,
or to want qualifying, as it must now, in 1849, take many
years to complete the arrangement and indexing. And in
fact it is so qualified in the preface to the first volume of
State Papers, page xx.

The following volumes have been printed in quarto by the above-mentioned Commission:—

1830. Vol. I. Divided into two parts:—

        Part I. Correspondence between Henry VIII. and Cardinal Wolsey; this however includes the Correspondence of other persons with Wolsey.

        Part II. is the Correspondence of Henry VIII. with his other Ministers. There is a brief calendar prefixed to each part, and a vocabulary at the end of the volume.

1834. Vols. II. and III., being the Correspondence between the Governments of England and Ireland; the first of these volumes contains the Correspondence from 1515 to 1538, and the other volume commences with part of 1538 to 1546. There is a brief calendar prefixed to each volume, and a vocabulary at the end of the latter volume.

1836. Vols. IV. and V. is the Correspondence relative to Scotland and the Borders. Vol. IV. embraces the years 1513 to 1534; and Vol. V. 1534 to 1546. There is a brief calendar prefixed to each volume, and a vocabulary at the end of Vol. V.

The Foreign Correspondence, which completes the series of papers of the time of Henry VIII., is in the hands of the printers, and will make six more quarto volumes, including a General Index of Reference to all the eleven volumes.

This Office, formerly annexed to the northern and southern divisions of the Secretariat of State, is under the control of the three Secretaries of State, but more especially of the Home Department, where application at present must be made by all persons desiring to inspect the documents.

A great change, however, has now been determined upon with respect to this Office. The Select Committee of the House of Commons on the Record Commission in 1836, p. xlii, recommended that, with a view to increased facility of access, and to unity of proceeding in publication, all State Papers not later than the conclusion of the Peace of Utrecht, and probably as late as the Accession of George the Third, should be placed in the custody of the Record Commission. The Report also from the Select Committee of the House of Commons on the Miscellaneous Expenditure in 1848, p. xvii., recommended a fusion of the office with the Public Record Office; and the Government had had under their consideration this matter in 1845, but in consequence of some obstacles being interposed nothing final was determined upon until 1848, when the following Treasury Minute was communicated to the Secretaries of State, and to the Master of the Rolls as head of the Public Record Office.

TREASURY MINUTE above referred to, dated
8th August 1848.

" Write to Lord Eddisbury, Mr. Hawes, and Mr. Lewis,
" and request that they will state to the three Secretaries
" of State, respectively, that my Lords have on several
" occasions had under their consideration the functions
" respectively performed by the State Paper Office and the
" Record Department, and they are of opinion that it would
" now be advisable to determine the course which ought
" finally to be adopted in reference to these two Offices.

" The State Paper Office is a repository for the reception
" and arrangement of the documents accumulating in the
" Offices of the Privy Council and the Secretaries of State,
" at whose disposal the documents are held, and no person
" is permitted to have access to these without an order from
" a Secretary of State. The establishment of the State
" Paper Office is as follows:—

　　" Keeper of the State Papers (Mr. Hobhouse).
　　" Deputy Keeper and First Clerk.
　　" Second Clerk, who has also a Salary as Secretary to
　　　　" the Commissioners for printing and publishing
　　　　" State Papers.
　　" Third Clerk.
　　" Two Extra Clerks.
　　" Four additional temporary Clerks.
　　" Housekeeper.
　　" Messengers.

" And including contingent expenses the estimated cost of
" the Office for the year 1848–9 amounts to £2,680.

" Commissions for publishing State Papers were issued in
" connexion with this Office in 1825 and 1840, under the
" authority of which the Letters of Henry VIII. have been

" printed, and Calendars are being prepared describing the
" contents of each document relating to the subsequent
" reigns, so that the public may be enabled to have ready
" access to the originals where more full information of their
" contents shall be required.

" The Record Department was established in the year
" 1838, under the authority of the Act 1 & 2 Vict. c. 94.
" The general superintendence is vested in the Master of
" the Rolls, who is assisted by the following Officers:—

" Deputy Keeper of Records.
" Secretary.
" Eight Assistant Keepers.
" Twenty-one Clerks.

" Besides certain offices and places of custody particularly
" mentioned in the Act, power is given to Her Majesty,
" with the advice of Her Privy Council, to order the Records
" deposited in any office, court, place, or custody other
" than those before mentioned to be placed under the same
" charge and superintendence, and their Lordships arranged
" with the Master of the Rolls that the management of the
" Records so transferred should be subject to regulations
" approved by the heads of the departments to which
" they respectively belong.

" Large quantities of papers which had accumulated in
" the Treasury, Admiralty, and other Offices, have accord-
" ingly been transferred to the Record Department, where
" they are not only taken proper care of, but are more easily
" consulted than they were previously to their transfer.

" As therefore Parliament has made provision for the
" whole of the State or Public Records of the country being
" brought under one central management, and this arrange-
" ment, besides its greater economy, would be productive
" of many obvious advantages, their Lordships are of opinion
" that no new appointments should be made to the separate
" Establishment of the State Paper Office; that on the
" retirement of the present Keeper of the State Papers the
" charge of that office should be transferred to the Master
" of the Rolls, and that the officers on the Establishment of
" the Record Department should after that be available for
" any duties for which they may be required in connexion
" with the arrangement, &c., of the documents deposited in
" the State Paper Office.

" In November 1845 it was arranged, in consequence of
" the want of accommodation in the State Paper Office, that
" when a sufficient period has elapsed to confer an historical

" character on particular classes of documents deposited in
" that office such documents should be transferred to the
" care of the department under the superintendence of the
" Master of the Rolls, where numerous contemporary and
" analogous records were already deposited, and the Master
" of the Rolls on that occasion made the following observa-
" tions in reply to some objections which had been offered
" to the transfer :—

" ' The Record Office would obey the directions of the
" Secretary of State to whose office any particular papers
" belonged, would afford the most perfect and convenient
" access to the officers of the same office, would send to
" the office the originals or copies of any papers whenever
" required, and would afford no access to other persons
" except by order of the office, or according to regulations
" approved by the office.

" ' In all such matters the Record Office would do pre-
" cisely as the State Paper Office would do or ought to do.'

" Their Lordships have now suggested that the State
" Paper Office should, on the retirement of the present
" Keeper, become a branch of the Record Department,
" under the superintendence of the Master of the ·Rolls, and
" they have made this proposal on the understanding that
" the conditions above described by Lord Langdale will be
" applied to this, as they have been to the present less com-
" plete arrangement.

" The operations of the Commission for printing and pub-
" lishing State Papers will properly cease after the publica-
" tion of the Papers of the time of Henry the Eighth, and
" when the State Paper Office and the Record Department
" shall have been consolidated, the printing of Calendars,
" Catalogues, and Indexes, as well as of such Records
" as may be approved by Her Majesty's Secretaries of
" State and the Lords of the Treasury, will be conducted
" under the superintendence of the Master of the Rolls, as
" directed by the 14th and 15th sections of the Record
" Act, 1 & 2 Vict. c. 94.

" State that in case Her Majesty's Secretaries of State
" shall signify their consent to the arrangements above
" described, my Lords will communicate with the Master of
" the Rolls, with a view to their being carried into effect at
" the proper time."

The assent of the Secretaries of State to the above pro-
position was communicated to the Master of the Rolls by
Treasury Letter, dated 14th September 1848, and the Master

of the Rolls, by his Letter dated 24th October following, consented to the arrangement. The advantages to be derived by the Government, and the public generally, by having one department only to refer to for legal and historical information must be obvious.

The State Papers or Documents may be said to be separated into ancient and modern. The ancient, down to the reign of Henry the Seventh inclusive, will generally be found in the Chancery, and in the custody of the Master of the Rolls; and those commencing with the reign of Henry the Eighth are at the State Paper Office, and now about to be brought together under one management. But it is lamentable to reflect on the dispersion of State Papers, commencing with the latter period, in other public departments and libraries; in the Public Record Department, in the British Museum, in the Lambeth Library, in the Libraries of the Universities, and in almost every private Library of note. A very fine collection remains in the Library of the Marquis of Salisbury, a catalogue of which is in the Public Record Office Library.

It would seem to be well worthy the expense and labour for the Government to cause to be formed in all departments, libraries, &c., where access could be obtained, a Calendar of all existing State Papers, and incorporate the same, with proper references, in the Calendars now forming in the State Paper Office.

Calendars alone can disclose the invaluable documents of the State Paper Office. The following view or heads of contents, however, will afford useful information.

The documents of this office may be divided into four great divisions, viz.—

1. Domestic Correspondence, subdivided: This includes the Correspondence with the Chief Officers and Chiefs of Ireland.

2. Colonies — including Foreign Possessions, from about William III.

3. Trade Papers.

4. Foreign — arranged in alphabetical order, commencing Abyssinia and ending Wirtemberg.

From Henry VIII.

The arrangement of each division is intended to be Alphabetical and Chronological, as follows:—

DOMESTIC CORRESPONDENCE

contains, amongst other matters, the following subjects, which, for convenience of reference, are here arranged in alphabetical order, and which were, for the most part, so arranged and classed, but it has been found expedient to incorporate many so classed into one general series.

ADMIRALTY AND NAVY Correspondence:—

> Ports and Havens, Transports, Voyages, and Discoveries.
>
> *See* also ' Secretaries' Letter Books.'
>
> Also 'Interregnum Papers.'
>
> Also in the Domestic Correspondence of the Foreign Department, under the head "Foreign Department," will be found, Admiralty Reports, 1745 to 1795; and Admiralty Communications, 1777 to 1805.
>
> Also among the Colonial, Admiralty Communications to Department of War and Colonies, 1794 to 1810.
>
> Also, Transport Office Communications, 1794 to 1815.
>
> Also, Mediterranean Fleet, 1761 to 1794, six volumes; and two volumes of Military Service, 1793 to 1794.

ADVENTURERS for Lands in Ireland.—*See* ' Ireland.'

ADVENTURERS, Merchant.

ALDERNEY.

ALIENS.

ARMS, Grants of.

BORDER Papers and Council of the North:—
> Those of the time of Hen. VIII. are printed.

CALAIS, and its Dependencies.

CINQUE PORTS.

COINAGE.

COMMISSIONS.

COMPOSITION Papers, temp. Interregnum.—*See* ' Interregnum Papers.'

CONFISCATED LANDS.—*See* ' Interregnum Papers.'

DOMESTIC CORRESPONDENCE—*continued.*

COUNCIL BOOKS of different Periods:—
    One very large volume, 1557–8 to May 1559.
    Of the Interregnum.
    Of the Lords Justices, 1695 to 1697, forming vols. i.
      and ii. of Papers called the 'Regency Papers.'
    Of Ireland, 1660–1675.

COUNCIL OF THE NORTH Papers:—
    These are blended with the Border Papers.

CRIMINAL Papers:—29 vols. bound, besides loose bundles.

CROMWELL'S Correspondence, temp. Hen. VIII.:—
    Brought from Chapter House.

CROWN LANDS, Papers relating to.

CUSTOMS, Matters relating to.

CYPHERS of Diplomatic Correspondence.

DECLARATIONS OF WAR:—
    In Sir Jos. Williamson's Collections.

DEEDS, Leases, Grants of Land and of Offices:—
    To which there is a Calendar of Persons and Places,
      and also an Index.

DELINQUENTS' ESTATES.—*See* 'Interregnum Papers.'

ECCLESIASTICAL Papers.

FENS.—Search under the Head 'Local History.'

FISHERIES.—*See* 'Trade, Fisheries,' &c.

FOREIGN DEPARTMENT, Papers relating to.—*See* 'Public
    Offices.'

FORFEITED ESTATES. — *See* 'Interregnum, Composition
    Papers,' p. 18.

FORTS AND GARRISONS.—*See* 'Military Correspondence.'

FUNERALS, Royal.

GRANTS. — *See* 'Sign Manuals,' 'Warrants,' 'Deeds,'
    'Heraldry.'

GUERNSEY and Jersey.

GUNPOWDER TREASON Papers, Jac. I.

HAVENS.—*See* 'Admiralty.'

HERALDRY:—
    Grants of Arms, Knighthood, Pedigrees, Peerage.

DOMESTIC CORRESPONDENCE — *continued.*

HOLLES, Denzel :—
Original Examination of, &c.

HOME Department :—
Secretaries' Letter Books.

HORSE, Master of the.—*See* 'Household.'

HOSPITAL and Foundation Schools. — Search under the Head 'Local History.'

HOUSEHOLD Papers :—
Lord Chamberlain's Office, Lord Steward's, Master of the Horse's, Office of Jewels, Office of Works.

INDENTURES of War, Original :—
Five volumes, Edw. III. to Hen. VII. These are the contracts entered into by the Sovereign of England with noblemen and others, for raising men when required, at a certain price.

INSTRUCTIONS to Ambassadors, &c.

INTERREGNUM Papers.
Council Books. Minutes and Orders :—
I. 16th Dec. 1653 to 30th March 1655. A large thick volume of Minutes and Orders, &c. The first entry is declaring Cromwell Protector, &c. To which volume there is an Index. At page 342 will be found the arrangements for electing Members to serve in Parliament, the numbers to be sent, &c.
II. 3d April 1655 to 21st March 1655-6. A large thick volume of Minutes and Orders, &c.; with an Index at the end.
III. 25th March 1656 to 13th June 1657. A large thick volume of Minutes and Orders, &c.; with an Index at p. 833.
This volume seems to have finished at p. 833; after which other matters are entered, such as Orders, Commissions, Declarations, Proclamations, Petitions, from 1656 to 14th Oct. 1657; with an Index also to this part of the volume.
IV. 13th July 1657 to 3d Aug. 1658. A thick volume of Minutes, Orders, &c.; with an Index at the end.
V. 11th Aug. 1659 to 25th Oct. 1659. A thin volume of Minutes, Orders, &c.; with an Index at the end.

B

DOMESTIC CORRESPONDENCE — *continued.*

Interregnum Papers — *continued.*

Acts of State 1654, 1655, Orders, Declarations, Proclamations. At the end is an Establishment of Forces in Field Garrison in England and Scotland. A Table of Contents at the end.

> *Note.*—The above entries are continued in vol. iii. of the Minute and Order Books, at the end.

Order Books, commencing 1643, ⎫
Ditto Army, 1643 to 1651,   ⎬ to which there are Indices.
Letter Books,   ⎭

Books of Warrants :—
  Admiralty,
  Ordnance,
  Money,
  Criminal and Passes.

Books of Committee of both Kingdoms —
  of Lords, ⎫
  of Commons, ⎪
  of Scotch affairs, ⎬ with their Order and Letter Books.
  of Lords and Commons, ⎪
  of Safety, ⎪
  of Foreign affairs, ⎭

Books of Commissioners for nomination of Commission Offices :—
  Reference to Committees.
  Negotiations with Sweden.
  Parliament.
  Abstracts and Petitions.
  Piedmontese, in the several Parishes of England and Wales.
  Jamaica, arrears due to several persons.

Various Books connected with the Government.

A mass of unarranged Revenue Papers.

Composition Papers, comprising two series :—
  The first, consisting of 113 volumes, which are the estates actually forfeited, to which there are Indices.
  The second, of 54 volumes, are the estates compounded for, to which there are Indices.
  There are also two large volumes of entries of Reports on Delinquents Estates.
  There are also 14 volumes of Petitions and Reports, in alphabetical order.

DOMESTIC CORRESPONDENCE — *continued.*

IRELAND.

The regular correspondence comes down to 1741, and is most valuable and interesting, of which that of the time of Henry VIII. is printed.

There are also 13 volumes, entitled " Adventurers for Lands in Ireland, during the time of Charles I. and the Commonwealth."

Also a Council Book, 1660 to 1675.

Also 20 volumes of English and Irish Petitions and Reports; to which there is a Calendar at the end of each volume.

Also one volume of ancient Maps, Plans, Surveys, &c., of Ireland.

One volume of County and Baronial Maps of Ulster, temp. Eliz.

One volume, a Plan of Ireland, containing Maps, Plans, names of principal Towns, Castles, Forts, chief Men of Ireland, names of Earldoms, Baronies, &c., Provinces, and their respective Counties.

There are also divers miscellaneous volumes, viz. —

1. Chronology of the Kings of Ireland to 1162.
2. A Note of the State of Ireland, with a device for the same, 16 pages, Henry VIII.

    Describes Ireland, according to the ancient description, as consisting of five parts: — 1, Ulster; 2, Connaught; 3, Two Munsters; 4, the other Munster; 5, Leinster. Signifies which of these obey the King's Law, and which do not; names of the Chiefs and Septs. Meaning of the English Pale, as embracing the obedient Shires. Tyrone's manner of conducting himself after the great benefits bestowed upon him by the King; comes to Dublin, probably once in a year, after being sent for two or three times; his dress. Ochonnor, the sorest adversary the King or his subjects ever had; his great power.

    Sets forth the policy of Englishmen towards the Irish, sometimes taking part with one and sometimes with another, so that none may get too strong, which when they do they generally prove what they are. The Irish when they are kept in awe and see the sword over them, will speak fair and make many behests, but when out of fear and have strength none are greater tyrants, their own will

DOMESTIC CORRESPONDENCE — *continued.*

Ireland — *continued.*

being Law. None should have too much strength.
Desmond will be obedient as long as he has his own
will. Great evil arises by giving Lands in the
Pale to the Irish, by reason of their servants going
to and fro, and observing the secrets of the country;
annuities would be better than lands; doubtful policy
of alluring Irishmen to England, &c., &c., &c.

3. A Declaration of the present state of the English
Pale, the causes of its misery, what Shires the Pale
consists of. 20 pages, temp. Eliz. (after 1590.)

States that the English Pale consisting of five
Shires,—1, Dublin ; 2, Meath; 3, Westmeath;
4, Kildare; 5, Louth (altogether not much larger
than Yorkshire in England),— is much wasted by
burning or otherwise by incursions of traitors and
rebels, and also by the great insolence, extreme
outrages, and disorders of the English paid soldiers;
great burthens laid upon the subjects by the Governors, Council, and Commanders; great suffering of
the Pale from the extortions of the soldiers exer-
cising great cruelty if not satisfied by their hosts;
their extortions, &c., have become so profitable
that some of the soldiers receive no pay from their
captains. Intolerable impositions, as well by the
State as by the principal commanders, for finding
men and horses in provisions, &c., which is levied
weekly upon the poor inhabitants without consent
of the nobility and gentlemen chiefly interested
therein : other oppressions by the soldiers in pay
of the English, many of whom have been traitors
pardoned, &c., who join cordially in order to ruin
the Pale better than they could by rebellion. Proclamations issued to prevent such outrages are of no
avail : the soldiers set forth that they do not properly receive their pay, which if they did they would
maintain themselves without grief to the country.

4. Base Monies, Eliz.—Sterling, Jac. I.

5. Rowland White's Reformation of Ireland. His
suggestions for,—addressed to Sir William Cecil,
Principal Secretary to Queen Eliz. (of the assumed
date 1570-1, March 23.)

Sets forth the capabilities of the country ; fruit-
ful of wood, water, grass, corn ground, and ines-

DOMESTIC CORRESPONDENCE — *continued.*

Ireland — *continued.*

timable treasures within the ground, good havens, &c., &c., the advantages of which are lost in desolation and waste by the idleness and disobedience of the people, living under no law, more brutish than reasonable, being savage and their counties fruitless; the great expenditure of Her Majesty has not brought quiet and civility, neither the correction of one hinders another from offending. The Reformation purposes to amend all these evils, its tendency being to serve God, and advance his word, to content and comfort the people, to redress and amend abuses, to strengthen and enrich the Realm, to forbid inconveniences and vanities, to extend the Queen's bountiful liberality, and to assure good order and faithful subjection.

The means,—

(1.) *Swearing of Irishmen to the Queen's Allegiance.* The Brehon Law to be abolished; the Irish to be sworn to be faithful to Her Majesty, Successors, &c., the universal subjection being thus begun, the Irish are to be admitted to participate, &c. in Her Majesty's affairs, &c.

(2.) *A Parliament.* The subjects being sworn, a Parliament is to be summoned according to the order observed in England, to be called from every part of the realm, &c. to enact as follows:

(3.) *An Act for Inheritors to take their Lands of the Queen.* In order to ensure right inheritance, all lands to be taken of the Queen by all those having a right of possession.

(4.) An Act ordaining that the next heir of legitimate blood shall inherit by lineal descent.

(5.) An Act restraining the exportation of green and untanned Hides, in order to employ the people in tanning the same, &c.

(6.) An Act restraining the exportation of Linen Yarn, in order to employ the idle in manufacturing the same, &c.

(7.) An Act restraining the exportation of Felt and Skins in order to encourage the manufacture and use of Gloves, &c.

(8.) An Act restraining the exportation of Wool in order to encourage the manufacture of Frieze, &c.

DOMESTIC CORRESPONDENCE — *continued.*

Ireland — *continued.*

(9.) An Act forbidding all Wines laden in strange bottoms to be discharged within the realm, and also forbidding all merchants, inhabitants of Ireland, to lade or freight in strange vessels, in order to encourage Shipbuilding, useful to the merchants and to the Crown in time of need.

(10.) An Act for inhabiting Waste Lands.

(11.) An Act for the Queen to have the proper right and possessions of all the Havens and Ports in the realm, in order to fortify, &c., the same, a great many of which remain at present in the hands of the Lords of the Country unfortified, &c.

(12.) Order for building Bulwarks in the Havens and Ports.

(13.) Order for building either sixteen holds or four principal Manors.

(14.) Order for building Castles in certain good Towns.

(15.) Order for farmers to be sent out of England to inhabit and till the Waste Grounds.

(16.) An Act forbidding Cosshery, Coyney, and Livery.

Cosshery.—When the Lord feasts any of his friends or strangers, the charge is borne amongst his poor tenants, &c.

Coyney.—The custom of Coyney is, that the poor husbandmen maintain the Kerne, Galloglasses, and other Warriors that the Lord keeps, who are disposed of among them, &c.

Livery.—Maintaining the Lord's Horses, &c.

(17.) An Act forbidding subjects to maintain men of War, *i. e.,* they must seek their right by law, and not by their own power, as they have been accustomed, &c. &c.

(18.) An Act forbidding the wearing of glybbed Heare, and all other vain apparel—ordaining the manner of England. The apparel of the Irish is described, and reasons given for altering the same.

DOMESTIC CORRESPONDENCE — *continued.*

Ireland — *continued.*

(19.) Foundation of 12 Free Schools.

The Scholars to be trained up to understand English and Latin, &c. &c.

(20.) Foundation of one University.

(21.) Appointment of 12 Preachers to preach in English, Latin, or Irish, as the audience may best understand.

(22.) The Foundation of 12 Hospitals for the Poor.

(23.) Three Presidents and Councils to be established, with 40 horsemen and 20 footmen each, in the three most needful places of the realm.

(24.) Appointment of Pleaders for the Poor, two to each of the Courts of the above-mentioned Presidents.

(25.) Justices of the Peace and Sheriffs to be appointed; the Country to be divided into Shires, &c.

(26.) Bailiffs, Constables, and other Officers to be appointed in every Shire, in order to further the Reformation, &c.

(27.) The appointment of four Provosts, in four quarters of the realm, to journey with 20 horsemen each in Circuit, through Munster, Leinster, Connaught, and Ulster, apprehending the evil doers, &c.

Note.—Accompanying each head are the reasons for the suggestion, and at the end of the book is a summary of the enormities of the realm; against each of which is placed the remedy as proposed by the Reformation; also the expense of carrying out the Reformation under the separate heads proposed for the said Reformation.

6. A Dialogue in four parts:—1, Outrages in Offaly or King's County; 2, Leinster; 3, Connaught and Ulster; 4, The Commonwealth of the County. (About 1598. 148 pages.) Describes the various outrages, by whom perpetrated; a sort of criticism on the proceedings in the above places, by way of dialogue.

B 4

Ireland — *continued.*

7. A View of the State of Ireland, by way of dialogue.
Eudoxus and Irenius, about 130 pages, very closely
written.

> *Note.* This is a very useful paper to consult by
> those who would write on Ireland, the mismanage-
> ment thereof, their customs, laws, &c. &c.; it pro-
> poses remedies, &c. &c. It is printed at the end of
> Spenser's works, and thus commences:—

> *Eudoxus.*—But if that country of Ireland whence
> you lately come be of so goodly and commodious a
> soil as you report, I wonder that no course is taken
> for the turning thereof to good uses and reducing
> that savage nation to better government and civility.

> *Irenius.*—Marry, so there have been divers good
> plots devised and wise counsel cast already about
> reformation of that realm. But they say it is the
> fatal destiny of that land that no purposes what-
> soever, meant for her good, will prosper or take
> effect, which whether it proceed from the very
> genius of the soil, or influence of the climate, or
> that Almighty God hath not yet appointed the time
> of their reformation, or that he reserveth her in this
> unquiet state still for some scourge which shall by
> her come into England, it is hard to be known, but
> yet much to be feared.

8. A Brief Discourse of Ireland, by Spenser, end of Eliz.

> Describes the causes which led to Tyrone's
> rebellion, how it grew for want of being properly
> met; original cause of the mischief happened in
> Munster; inexperience of the Undertakers of the
> Queen's Lands in Munster, being but husbandmen
> trained up in peace, &c. The Irish hate the English
> for two causes, viz.:—1. Because they, the Irish,
> have ever been brought up licentiously, living each
> as he listeth, which they esteem half-happiness, so
> that to be brought into better order they account
> to be restrained of their liberty. 2. Because they
> naturally hate the English; the cause of this original
> hate is that they were conquered of the English,
> the memory whereof is yet fresh among them; they
> desire revenge and recovery of their lands. It is

Ireland — *continued.*

suggested that in the first institution these prejudices should have been provided against; the old buildings should have been pulled down before any new were erected, and not to have thought to have patched them together in an inequality of state; suggests what ought to have been done; priests preaching against the Queen, &c. &c. Question suggested whether it would be better and easier for Her Majesty to subdue Ireland or to reform it; of these two, that must needs be a better and easier way which may be done with less charge, peril, and time. *Reason*:—The assumption then is that it will be less charge, less peril, and less spending of time, to subdue it altogether than to go about to reform it. Proof of the reason, &c. &c.

9. Mountjoy's Discourse on Ireland, 1601.

Describes the country as abounding with all the sustenance for life, as corn, cattle, fish and fowl, mines, quarries of stone and marble, breeding a people of excellent temper, if it were governed by virtue. The ancient obstacle to reducing it to civility was, that after it was inhabited by the first conquerors, their inheritance, for want of issue male, descended to women who, many of them married into England, deprived the land of a lord to be resident upon it; also the divisions of the Houses of York and Lancaster withdrew many of the nobility into England, and bred a war between the rest, &c. &c. The later cause of the general revolt and prevailing of the rebels was the corruptions of the magistrates sent hither, and weakness of their counsels, directed most to private and not public ends; and continual dissensions of the English inhabitants; insufficiency of particular commanders. Mountjoy describes his own proceedings against the rebels, which would have been still more successful had he not been overruled; a grievance that the soldiers are not paid in money and victuals, and to abolish the matter of apparel, which is full of inconvenience.

10. State of Ireland when Essex was appointed Lord Lieutenant, 1599.

DOMESTIC CORRESPONDENCE — *continued.*

Ireland — *continued.*

11. Cause of Tyrone's rebellion; four pages.

12. Advice in mustering to avoid deceit (by Lane), 1593.

13. A curious miscellaneous volume, with Table of Contents, in which will be found what Records are in the Tower concerning Ireland.

> *Note.*—There are at the Signet Office numerous Books containing copies of the Sovereign's Letters transmitted from this country to the several Lord Lieutenants or other Chief Governors of Ireland on public business, from 1626 to the present time, authorizing him to pass Letters Patent under the Great Seal of Ireland, and comprehending Patents of Inventions, Grants of Offices, Creations, &c. Irish Letters authorizing the expenditure of money originate in the Treasury, and are countersigned by the Lords.—*See* First Rep. of Com. on Fees, 1837, p. 63. These were directed to be entered at the Signet Office by the Royal Mandates of Car. I. and II. There appear to be some chasms, including one from 1645-6 to June 1660, since which they seem to be complete. There are Indices to them, with chasms to 1776, from which time they are complete. *See* Record Report, 1837, p. 80, second column, bottom.

JENKINS, Sir Leoline :—

The collection of Papers, Foreign and Domestic, collected by him during the time he was Secretary of State to Car. II. and bequeathed by him to the State Paper Office, consists of Correspondence with the different Foreign Powers, 1673 to 1684; the Domestic part consists of four volumes of Petitions, and one volume relating to Duke of Monmouth, Lord Russell, Earl of Essex, Algernon Sydney, &c. 1683-4.

> *Note.*—The Foreign portion is in course of incorporation with the regular Foreign Correspondence. *See* " Separate Collections," p. 59.

JERSEY.

JEWELS, Office of.—*See* ' Household.'

JOINTURES of the Queens of England:—Hen. VIII. to Jac. I.

DOMESTIC CORRESPONDENCE — *continued.*

KINGS' Letter Books.

KNIGHTHOOD.—*See* 'Heraldry.'

LAW PAPERS :—
> Eight volumes bound, 1684–1768, and some unbound, containing matters concerning the Court of Star Chamber, Court of Wards and Liveries, Proceedings in Law Courts, Reports and Opinions in Law Cases.

LEASES.—*See* 'Deeds.'

LETTER BOOKS of Kings, Queens, and Secretaries of State.

LICENCES to Preach.

LIEUTENANCY :—
> Matters relating to, in Sir J. Williamson's Collection.
> Matters concerning Lord Lieutenants and Deputy Lieutenants of Counties, among the Militia and Military Papers.

LISLE, Lord. Lord Deputy of Calais.—His correspondence, temp. Henry VIII., brought from the Chapter House.

LOANS.—*See* 'Revenue.'

LOCAL HISTORY.—24 bound volumes. Counties alphabetically arranged.

LORD CHAMBERLAIN'S Department.—*See* 'Household.'

LORD STEWARD'S Department.—*See* 'Household.'

LORDS JUSTICES.—*See* 'Regency Papers.'

MANUFACTURES.—*See* 'Trade.'

MARGARET, Princess :—
> Her Journey, 1502. One volume, in the Scotch Press (Foreign).

MARLBOROUGH, Duke of.—*See* the Foreign Correspondence, Flanders, Germany, &c.

MARY, Queen of Scots :—
> Several volumes of Papers relating to her.

MASTER OF THE HORSE.—*See* 'Household,'

MERCHANT ADVENTURERS.

MILITARY CORRESPONDENCE :
> Camp Letters, Commissions, Forts and Garrisons, Militia, Musters, Muster Rolls, Ordnance. — *See* also under the Colonial arrangement, commencing p. 34.

DOMESTIC CORRESPONDENCE — *continued.*

MINES.

MINT, Coinage, &c.

MONMOUTH, Duke of:—
   Papers relating to him.—*See* under the head 'Jenkins.'

MUSTER ROLLS.—*See* 'Military Correspondence.'

NAVAL.—*See* 'Admiralty.'

OATHS and Obligations :—
   Forming part of Sir J. Williamson's Collection.

ORDERS IN COUNCIL.—*See* 'Privy Council Orders,' 'Inter-regnum Papers,' 'Petitions and Reports and Orders in Council, 1660–1678,' 20 volumes, 'Lords Justices,' two volumes, 1695–1697, being the first two volumes of Regency Papers, marked 'Whitehall.'

ORDERS, Book of, against Forestalling :—
   These Orders went to inquire, what lands grew corn? who owned it? how many persons they had to feed? how many apprentices? what markets their corn was taken to? who bought it, &c. &c., as a measure against forestallers.   The first book of this kind was issued by Queen Elizabeth, King James amended it, and Charles I. made a new Book of Orders.   To the Book of Orders of Elizabeth and James no returns have as yet been discovered; but to that of Charles I. the returns were found in the State Paper Office, and are about the date of 1631; these returns were some years since sent to the Secretary of State's Office, and probably now are to be found in the Statistical Department of the Board of Trade; but more have since been found, and remain in the State Paper Office.

ORDNANCE.—*See* 'Military.'

PAMPHLETS and Tracts.

PETITIONS and References :—Eliz. to Car. II., 41 volumes.

PETITIONS and Reports during the Interregnum :—14 volumes, in alphabetical arrangement.

PETITIONS and Reports, Charles II. :—12 volumes.

PETITIONS and Reports and Orders in Council :—
   English and Irish, 1660–1678, 20 volumes; a calendar at the end of each volume.
   There are also four volumes of Petitions collected by Sir Leoline Jenkins, temp. Charles II.

DOMESTIC CORRESPONDENCE — *continued.*

PETITIONS and Reports for Scotland. — 1720–1725. (*See* ' Warrants,' Scots.)

PLANTATIONS.—*See* under the Colonial and Trade arrangements, pp. 34–39.

PLOTS.—*See* ' Gunpowder Treason Papers,' ' Rye House Plot,' and ' Scotland.'

PORTS and Havens.

POST OFFICE.

PRECEDENCY.—*See* ' Styles and Titles.'

PRISONERS OF WAR.

PRIVY COUNCIL BOOKS.—*See* ' Council Books.'

PRIVY COUNCIL ORDERS.

PRIVY SEALS and Privy Seal Writs, Privy Seal and Signet Dockets.

There are original Privy Seal Writs from 1216 to 1547 ; these are part of the Records transmitted to the State Paper Office by order of the House of Lords in 1770, and are Exchequer documents. There is a calendar, in a preface to which is given an account where these documents were found, and their progress from place to place, until they were lodged, as stated above, in the State Paper Office.

There are also Privy Seal and Signet Dockets, in bundles, Eliz. to Car. II., both inclusive ; these are kept under the general head of ' Warrants.'

Also, Copies of Warrants or Privy Seals, Eliz. and Jac. I.

Also several bound volumes of Dockets of Privy Seals or Sign Manuals, Jac. I. and Car. I.

See also ' Sign Manuals.'

PROCLAMATIONS.

PUBLIC OFFICES.

Papers relating to Exchequer, Post Office, Secretary of State's Office, State Paper Office, Foreign Department, and Treasury.

QUEENS' Letter Books.

QUEENS of ENGLAND :—

Jointures, from Hen. VIII. to Jac. II.

DOMESTIC CORRESPONDENCE — *continued*.

RALEIGH, Sir Walter :—

Papers concerning him when a Captain in Ireland.
See the Irish Chronological Memoranda, or Notes
under the head 'Raleigh,' temp. Eliz., in the State
Paper Office.

There is a Warrant giving the Government of Kerry
and Clanmorris in Ireland to Ralph Lane, in consideration of his ready undertaking the voyage to
Virginia for Sir Walter Raleigh,   *See* Irish Correspondence, 8th February 1564–5.

Copy of Sir Walter Raleigh's Commission to go to
South America, Jac. I., in a folio Warrant or Privy
Seal Book, p. 209.

See also vol. 234 of Sir J. Williamson's Miscellaneous
Collection.

In a volume of Sir J. Williamson's Collection, marked
'Collection of Letters, Speeches, &c.' in small 4to.
several matters relating to Raleigh will be found,
viz. his letter to his wife, November 1618; verse
made the day before his execution; his account
of his voyage to Guiana; his letters to the King,
Oct. 1618; his apology, at p. 54; his death, p. 57.

REBELLION Papers.— *See* 'Scotland.'

RECORDS :—

A mass of copies of Records in Sir J. Williamson's
Collection.

RECUSANTS :—

Composition for their Estates. — *See* 'Interregnum
Papers.'

REGENCY Papers :—

Marked 'Hanover' and 'Whitehall'; those marked
'Hanover' being the Correspondence from Hanover
during the time of the Regency, and the King being
at Hanover, 1719 to 1755; those marked 'Whitehall'
contain the Correspondence from England to Hanover
during the same period; the first two volumes of the
latter are the Council Books of the Lord Justices,
and their Minutes and Orders; vol. 3 commences the
Correspondence from England to Hanover.

For the other Hanover Correspondence, see 'Hanover,'
under the head 'German Princes' in the Foreign
arrangement, p. 44.

DOMESTIC CORRESPONDENCE — *continued.*

REVENUE :—Viz., Crown Lands, Woods and Forests, Customs, Loans, Subsidies, and Mines.

ROBES, Office of.— *See* 'Household.'

ROYAL LETTERS :—
> These are described under the Foreign or Diplomatic arrangement.

RYE HOUSE PLOT, Papers concerning the.

SCHOOLS.

SCOTLAND.
> The early correspondence to 1603 forms part of the Foreign arrangement, being to that time a Foreign country, from which period it forms part of the Domestic arrangement, King James having then succeeded to the Crown of England. There are five volumes of Correspondence, 1603 to 1645–6 ; the first three volumes contain correspondence ; vol. 4 is marked 'Committee of both Kingdoms ;' vol. 5 is 'Muster Roll of the Scots Army, January 1645–6.' There is a volume also dated 1667–8 to 1674 ; then commences Correspondence from 1707–8, including the Correspondence in various English counties touching the Scottish Rebellions. And there are certain Rebellion and Treason Papers from about or before Geo. I. to 1745, and papers of later date having reference to the Rebellion of 1745, &c.
>
> Union of England and Scotland.—Papers connected with the proposition, Jac. I. to Car. II.
>
> A Journal of the Proceedings relative to the Union in the reign of Queen Anne, one very large volume.

SECRETARIES' Letter Books.
> The Domestic or Home Department, from about 1674 to about 1761.
>
> The Secretaries' Letter Books relating to Foreign affairs will be found in the Foreign arrangement, p. 50.

SELDEN, John, arrested by order of Charles I., 1628–9 ; original examination of, &c., among Criminal Papers.

SEQUESTRATIONS.— *See* 'Interregnum Papers.'

SETTLEMENTS, Marriage.— *See* 'Jointures.'

SICK and Wounded Prisoners of War.—Among the Admiralty Papers.

DOMESTIC CORRESPONDENCE — *continued.*

SIGNINGS (Hen. VIII.)—By Stamp, 1545 to 1547.

SIGN MANUALS, Grants, Warrants, 1609 to 1645. 18 bound volumes.

SQUIRE (or Squyer) Edward, executed for poisoning the Saddle of Queen Elizabeth, &c. The papers concerning this transaction to be found among the Criminal Papers. —(*See* also Baga de Secretis, Part 55, in the Public Record Office.)

STAR CHAMBER.—*See* 'Law Papers.'

STATE PAPER OFFICE.—A Collection of Papers relating to the history, &c. of the State Paper Office. This collection is in the Treaty Press.

STEPNEY.—*See* 'Separate Collections,' page 55.

STEWARD, Lord High.—*See* 'Household.'

STYLES and Titles.—*See* Secretaries' Letter Books marked 'Styles and Titles, 1627, 1628.' Also Sir J. Williamson's Collections.

SUBSIDIES.—*See* 'Revenue.'

SYDNEY, Algernon, Papers relating to.—*See* 'Jenkins.'

TRACTS and Pamphlets, a collection of.

TRADE, Fisheries, and Foreign Plantations. A great number of volumes 1542 to 1761. These form a collection of Papers collected from the different classes of Correspondence and documents upon the above subjects. Whether the Foreign and other Correspondence has been injured by forming such a Collection, and whether many of them ought not to be returned to the series from whence taken, especially those taken from the Foreign Correspondence, has probably yet to be considered.

  There is also a very large early collection of papers belonging to the Board of Trade and Plantations. *See* page 39.

TRANSPORTS, matters relating to, among the Admiralty Papers.

UNION with Scotland, Papers relating to.—*See* 'Scotland.'

UNIVERSITIES, Papers relating to, among the Ecclesiastical.

DOMESTIC CORRESPONDENCE — *continued.*

VALENTINE, Benjamin, arrested by order of Car. I.; original examination, &c. Among the Criminal Papers.

VATICAN Papers.—A collection of Transcripts relating to this country, made from the Registries and MSS. of the Vatican, chiefly relating to ecclesiastical matters, from about 1087 to about 1756. These, for what reason does not appear, have been transferred from the State Paper Office to the British Museum.

These transcripts were prepared by the Abbé Marine. By an arrangement with the British Government, through Mr. Wm. Hamilton, in 1825, the Abbé was to be paid at per volume, and to have a pension for life after the production of the documents, to the number of 6000, making about 30 volumes, and costing about 720*l.* Some of these papers have been printed among the State Papers published by the Commissioners for printing and publishing State Papers. Those writing on ecclesiastical matters could make great use of them. Should a new edition of the Monasticon come out, these papers ought to be consulted: for in the letters of Innocent III. are to be found the names of many persons, churches, bishops, abbots, and archdeacons, of which there is little knowledge; also the ancient names and descriptions of the lands, churches, abbeys, &c.; sometimes the incomes of the benefices, exemptions from tythe, privileges of certain monasteries, and many other matters of which there is no knowledge, except from the letters of Innocent III.

VIRGINIA (America), Smith's account of.—*See* vol. 28. First Series of Sir Jos. Williamson's Collection; the Books in the Colonial arrangement, pp. 35. 37.; and 'Raleigh, Sir Walter.'

VISITATIONS.—Among the Ecclesiastical Papers.

VOYAGES of Discovery, Papers relating to; among the Admiralty Papers; also in Sir J. Williamson's Collection.

WAR, Declarations of.—*See* Sir J. Williamson's Collection.

WAR OFFICE, Papers relating to; among the Military Papers.

WAR, original Indentures of.—*See* 'Indentures.'

WARDS and Liveries, Court of.—*See* 'Law Papers.'

DOMESTIC CORRESPONDENCE — *continued.*

WARRANTS :—

　English Warrant Books 1661 to 1711.
　Scots 　　„ 　　„ 　 1670 to 1714.
　There are also three Entry Books of Warrants, Privy
　　Seals, &c., temp. Eliz. and Jac. I.
　Also Privy Seal and Signet Dockets, in bundles, Eliz.
　　to Car. II. inclusive.
　See also 'Privy Seals' and 'Sign Manuals.'
　See among the Interregnum Papers.

WILLIAMSON, Sir Joseph.—*See* his collection of Papers,
　page 60.

WOLSEY, Cardinal :—

　His Correspondence has been printed and published by
　　the Commissioners for printing and publishing State
　　Papers, and forms the first volume of their pub-
　　lications, as before stated in p. 10.

WOODS and FORESTS.—*See* 'Revenue.'

WORKS, Office of.—*See* 'Household.'

---

2. COLONIES AND FOREIGN POSSESSIONS.

AMERICA and WEST INDIES, 1689 to 1783, viz.—

Date.	First Series, 93 Volumes.	Vol.
— to 1758	Amherst, General.—*See* Louisburg.	66 f.
1759–1764	„　　　　 *See* also vols...	73 to 84
1718–1746	Bahama Islands	49–50
1689–1752	Barbadoes	29–34 a. b.
1689–1751	Bermuda	42–64
— to 1758	Boscawen, Admiral.—*See* Louisburg.	
1710–1713	Canada Expedition	51
— to 1746	„　　 and Governors	56
1746–1749	Cape Breton	58
1689–1752	Caribbee Islands, Leeward	45–48
1711–1745	Carolina, North	19 a. b.
1715–1751	„　　　 South	16. 17 a. b. 18
1740–1743	Carthagena Expedition	54–55
	Connecticut.—*See* New England.	
	Expeditions.—*See* Canada.	
	„　 ·　　 *See* Carthagena.	
	„　 ·　　 *See* Porto Bello.	

COLONIES and FOREIGN POSSESSIONS — *continued.*

America and West Indies — *continued.*

Date.	First Series, 93 Volumes.	Vol.
1708–1713	Fisheries, Papers relating to, between France and England.................. }	52
	France.—*See* Fisheries.	
1735–1751	Georgia	20–22
1743–1761	Governors.—From Governors, America	59–66
1753–1763	„ To Governors...........	66 a. b. c. d.
— to 1746	„ From Governors, West Indies .... }	56
1757–1763	„ To Governors	66 e.
1755–1764	„ Various Governors, &c.	67–84
1761–1763	Grenada and Martinique	87
1758–1763	Guadaloupe	85–86
— to 1753	Jamaica................................	35–41
	Leeward Caribbee.— *See* Caribbee.	
— to 1758	Louisburg, Admiral Boscawen } *See* „ General Amherst.. }	{ 66 f. { 73–84.
1761–1763	Martinique	87
1689–1740	Maryland................................	23
1710–1740	Massachusets Bay	5
1720–1747	Miscellaneous	57
1756–1761	„ Secret and Miscellaneous	66 h.
1755–1764	„ Various persons, Governors, &c...................... }	67–84
1689–1749	New England : — Containing New Hampshire, Massachusets, Rhode Island, Connecticut, Vermont, Maine, part of Massachusets ...... }	1–4
1706–1752	Newfoundland...........................	27–28
1711–1752	New Hampshire	5
1728–1752	New Jersey	{ 12 a. b. { 13 a. b.
1696–1752	New York..............................	6–11
1711–1745	North Carolina..........................	19 a. b.
1716–1752	Nova Scotia	25 a. b. 26
1738–1770	Orders in Council.— *See* also Transports .... }	88–93
1709–1746	Pennsylvania	24
1740–1743	Porto Bello Expedition	54–55
1759	Quebec	73
1709–1742	Rhode Island	5
1715–1751	South Carolina	16. 17 a. b. 18
1710–1712	Transports, &c.	53
1694–1752	Virginia	14–15

COLONIES and FOREIGN POSSESSIONS—*continued.*

America and West Indies — *continued.*

Date.	Second Series, 258 Volumes.	Vol.
— to 1767	Answers to Circulars..................	161–162
1767–1780	Bahama and Turks Island............	213–214
1767–1782	Barbadoes..............................	199–200
1767–1781	Bermuda	215–216
1762–1777 1767–1782 1768–1781 }	Carolina, North	{ 88–96 176–179 249
1762–1777 1767 1768–1782 }	„ South	{ 97–103 180–181 250
1767	Circulars.—*See* Answers.	
1758	Commissioners for quieting disorders in America. *See* Correspondence. *See* also 'America,' under the Foreign Arrangement. Vol. I.	} 165–167
	Correspondence with Civil Officers of Provinces, now the United States, during the Rebellion. *See* also Commissioners..................	} 163–164
1770–1779	Dominica.	
1763–1786 1767–1781 1768–1783 }	Florida, East............	{ 112–125 189–191 252
1763–1781 1766–1781 1766–1781 }	„ West.........................	{ 126–140 192–194 253
1761 1767–1782 1768–1782 }	Georgia.................................	{ 104–111 182–184 251
1766–1781	Grenada.................................	201–205
1767–1782	Jamaica.................................	195–198
1766–1782	Leeward Islands	208–211
1762–1774 1766–1776 }	Massachusets Bay......................	{ 41–49 234–237 254
1763–1781 1769–1782 1783 }	Military.................................	{ 1–33 168–175 246–248
1782–1783	Naval Commanders	34
1767–1781	Newfoundland...........................	230–231

COLONIES and FOREIGN POSSESSIONS — *continued.*

America and West Indies — *continued.*

Date.	Second Series, 258 Volumes.	Vol.
1762 1767–1777	New Hampshire	35–40 240–241 256
1763 1767–1781 1768–1782	New Jersey......................	64–70 238–239 255
1762–1780 1767–1781	New York......................	50–63 242–245 257
	North Carolina.— *See* Carolina.	
1766–1781	Nova Scotia......................	227–229
1760–1784 1766–1781	Plantations, General	141–158 221–226
	Precis......................	159–160
1762–1777 1766–1775	Proprieties......................	71–78 185–186 259
1766–1781	Quebec	217–220
1770–1781	St. John's, Island of	232–233
1776–1780	St. Vincent's Island......................	206–207
	South Carolina.— *See* Carolina.	
1767–1780	Turks Island......................	213–214
1762–1777 1777 1768–1776	Virginia	79–87 187–188 258

There are also six volumes marked ' Military Papers, West Indies,' 1778–1784.

Ditto two volumes, marked ' Nova Scotia,' 1782–1787.

Ditto one volume, ditto ' America,' 1790 to 1791.

Ditto one volume, ditto 1794.

There is also a mass of unarranged and West India Papers, viz. — North and South Carolina, Maryland, Pennsylvania, Georgia, Newfoundland, Bermuda, Nevis, Bahama, and Leeward Islands, New England, Massachusets Bay, New Hampshire, Rhode Island, New York, Virginia, Jamaica, Barbadoes, Antigua, Petitions and Memorials, Military, &c.

COLONIES and FOREIGN POSSESSIONS—*continued.*

AMERICA, South:—
> One volume, marked ' Demerara, Essequibo, Berbice, 1781–1784.'
> There are about 50 volumes in Dutch.
> Essequibo and Demerara, about 1700 to 1791.
> Also Surinam Population Returns.

ANHOLT. — One volume, 1809–1813 ; one volume Military Returns, 1812–1814.

CORSICA.—1794 to 1796–7, about seven volumes.

CORSICA and TOULON.—Correspondence of the Commissioners at Toulon and Corsica, 1793—1794, two volumes.

EAST INDIES :—
> Papers relating to, 1581–1783, seven volumes. There is a Calendar to this Series.
>   ,,   1776–1787, two volumes.
>   ,,   1793, four volumes.

GIBRALTAR.—1705–1755, four volumes; 1711–12 to 1767, four volumes.

MALTA.—*See* ' Press Copies,' p. 39; also ' Malta,' under the Foreign arrangement.

MEDITERRANEAN FLEET.—1761–1794.

MEDITERRANEAN MILITARY.—1794–1795.

MILITARY and NAVAL Returns :—
> Madras, 1811–1815.
> Madeira, 1810–1814.
> Bombay, 1811–1812.
> Bengal, 1811–1814.
> Gibraltar, 1810–1816.
> Heligoland, 1810–1815.
> Africa, Sierra Leone, &c., 1810–1817,
> Bahamas, 1810–1816.
> Jamaica, 1810–1811.
> Honduras, 1810–1816.
> Isles of Bourbon and France, 1810–1816.
> Ceylon, 1811–1817.
> New South Wales, 1811–1814.
> Canadas, 1812–1815, &c. &c.

MINORCA.—1742 to 1785.

COLONIES and FOREIGN POSSESSIONS—*continued.*

PASSPORTS to the Colonies.—1806–1815, 21 volumes.

PRESS COPIES of Letters sent from the Department of War and Colonies to the different Public Offices and Foreign Possessions, from about 1811 to 1815, viz. to the Public Offices, Army in the Netherlands, Gibraltar, Hanover, Heligoland, Ionian Islands, Malta, St. Helena, Sicily, &c.

RETURNS.—*See* 'Military and Naval Returns.'

SENEGAMBIA —1764–1787, Eight volumes.

TANGIERS.— *See* 'Sir Leoline Jenkins' Collection,' 1671–1684, p. 59.

TOULON.—*See* 'Corsica and Toulon.'

---

3. TRADE AND PLANTATIONS.

There is a large series of Papers of some hundreds of volumes, formerly belonging to the Old Board of Trade and Plantations, under similar heads to those of the Colonies and Foreign Possessions.

---

4. FOREIGN OR DIPLOMATIC.

Being the Correspondence, &c. with and relating to Foreign Powers, under alphabetical arrangement, generally commencing in the reign of Henry VIII. to about 1810, the subsequent Correspondence remaining at the Foreign Office.

ABYSSINIA.— One volume, marked 'Lord Valentia and Mr. Salt, Sept. 1800 to Dec. 1813.'

ALGIERS.—*See* 'Barbary States.'

AMBASSADORS :—

    Credentials.—*See* the Correspondence generally, 'Secretaries' Letter Books,' and 'Royal Letters.'

    Instructions.—*See* the Correspondence generally, 'Sir Jos. Williamson's Collection,' 'Royal Letter Books,' and 'Secretaries' Letter Books.'

FOREIGN or DIPLOMATIC CORRESPONDENCE —*continued.*

Ambassadors — *continued.*

> *Ceremonies, Proceedings, Observances, &c.*—*See* Sir Jos.
> Williamson's Collection, under the head 'Styles and
> Titles,' p 82.
>
> There is an Index and Notes of the time when Ambas-
> sadors were sent to and returned from Foreign Parts,
> being one of Sir Jos. Williamson's Collection, marked
> 'Diplomatic Index and Notes—Ambassadors.'
>
> There is also another large volume, containing notices
> of the time of departure and return, credentials, &c.
> of Ambassadors, formed by Mr. Lechmere, the Deputy
> Keeper of State Papers.
>
> *See* also Stepney's Collection, pp. 55–58.

AMERICA :—

> This Correspondence is separated from that of the
> Colonies from the time the United States became
> an Independent State. It consists of 96 volumes,
> 1779 to 1810. The first volume is 'Commissioners
> for restoring Peace, 1779–1782.'

ANSPACH.—*See* 'German Princes.'

AUGSBURGH.—*See* 'German Princes—Ratisbon.'

AUSTRIA :—

> For the early Correspondence, *See* 'Germany—Vienna.'
> The Correspondence, marked 'Austria,' commences
> 1781 to 1814. 114 volumes.
> There is one volume marked 'Trieste, 1756 to 1806.'

BARBARY STATES :—

> Algiers, 1601–1799. 10 volumes.
> Morocco, Sallee, &c., 1574–1772. Eight volumes.
> Tripoli, 1590–1766. Three volumes.
> Tunis, 1622–1769. Four volumes.
>
> For Correspondence also with the Barbary States, search
> the papers marked 'Mediterranean Fleet,' in the Colonial
> arrangement; also the Corsica Correspondence in the
> Colonial arrangement.

BAVARIA.—*See* 'German Princes—Bavaria.'

BRANDENBURG.—*See* 'German Princes—Brandenburg.'

BRUNSWICK.—1785–1810. Two volumes.

> For the early Correspondence, *See* 'German Princes—
> Hanover,' p. 44.

FOREIGN or DIPLOMATIC CORRESPONDENCE — *continued.*

CASSEL.— *See* 'German Princes—Cologne, Hanover, Hesse Cassel.'

CLEVE.— *See* ' German Princes—Ratisbon.'

COLOGNE :—
A mass of Papers relating to the Treaty of Cologne.
See ' German Princes —Cologne ;' ' Sir J. Williamson's Collection,' pp. 77–79.

COURLAND AND HOLSTEIN :—1645–1682. These formed part of Sir Leoline Jenkins' Collection.— *See* 'Denmark.'

CYPHERS.—A Collection of Diplomatic Cyphers.

DENMARK:—There are about 200 volumes of Correspondence, 1533 to 1810.— *See* also Sir Leoline Jenkins' Collection.

DUNKIRK :—
There are nine volumes of Correspondence, &c. 1712 to 1743–4.

> *Note.* Dunkirk was surrendered to England by Treaty 1658, and Cromwell made Lockhart Governor. It was sold by Car. II. to France 1662, the negotiations for which began in July and ended in October 1662. It was delivered up to the British, July 1712, as a security for what the French had promised to do in their negotiations.
>
> For the various Treaties respecting the demolition of the fortifications, see the Treaties of Utrecht 1713, Triple League 1716–7, Aix-la-Chapelle 1748, Treaty with France 1762. But by the 18th Article of the Preliminaries of Peace, signed at Versailles 20th Jan. 1783, the King of Great Britain consented to the abrogation of all the Articles relative to Dunkirk from the Treaty of Utrecht to the (then) present time.

EGYPT.—1786–1810.

EXTRA-PROVINCIAL :—
Under this title will be found duplicates of Correspondence, Despatches, &c. sent by the British Ministers and Agents at Foreign Courts to Hanover during the time of the King being there. These will probably hereafter be incorporated with the regular Correspondence of the different countries. They are from about 1725 to 1755, and will in many cases fill up chasms.

FOREIGN or DIPLOMATIC CORRESPONDENCE — *continued.*

FLANDERS : —

A very fine collection of Correspondence and Papers, commencing temp. Hen. VIII. down to about 1810. These were formerly separated into divers collections and series, which have been collected together and incorporated and arranged in one chronological series.

As to the time of separation of the United Provinces (or Holland) from Flanders, a few observations are offered under the head ' Holland.'

FLORENCE.— *See* ' Tuscany.'

FOREIGN DEPARTMENT : —

Under the above head will be found the Domestic Correspondence of the Foreign Department with the various Offices connected with the Government, viz.

Vol. 1. Marked Great Britain, Admiralty Reports, 1745–1795.

    2. Ditto, Admiralty Communications, 1777–1805.

    3. Ditto, Treasury ditto, 1768–1806.

    4. Ditto, Home Department ditto, 1783–1806.

    5. Ditto, Post Office ditto, 1781–1806.

    6. Ditto, Council Office ditto, 1781–1806.

    7. Ditto, War Office ditto, 1777–1805.

    8. Ditto, Memorials, Certificates, &c., 1781–1801.

    9. Ditto, Applications, Recommendations, and Solicitations for Consulships South of Europe, 1793–1802.

    10, 11. Missing.

    12, 13, 14, 15, and 16. Marked Miscellaneous, 1802–1810.

    17. Antonio Perez, 1808–1810. This volume is a series of political letters, by the Ghost of Antonio Perez, touching French politics towards Spain, &c.

Note.—Similar communications from the different offices connected with the Government to the Department of War and Colonies will be found under the Colonial arrangement.

FOREIGN MINISTERS.— *See* ' Ministers—Foreign.'

FRANCE : —There is an immense number of volumes of Correspondence, Papers, Advices, &c.

FOREIGN or DIPLOMATIC CORRESPONDENCE—*continued.*

FRANKFORT.—*See* 'German Princes—Frankfort.'

GENEVA.—*See* 'Switzerland.'

GENOA.—1684–1803. 43 volumes.

GERMAN PRINCES AND STATES :—

Anspach. — One volume marked ' Baron Seckendorff, 1749 to 1752.'

Augsburgh.—*See* Ratisbon.

Bavaria.—*Note.* The Elector became King by Treaty of Presburg 1805.

1746–1750.—*See* Frankfort and Munich.

1746–1759.—*See* Munich.

1766–1780.—*See* Ratisbon.

1781–1810.—38 vols.

Brandenburg.—There is a volume marked ' Newburg and Brandenburgh, 1614–1618,' under the head 'Germany, Vienna ': —

See Sir Leoline Jenkins' Collection, 1673–1682, p. 59.

See Prussia. *Note.*—The Elector became King of Prussia 1701.

Brunswick.—*See* Hanover, 1785–1810. Two volumes.

Cassel.—*See* Cologne, Hanover, and Hesse Cassel.

Cleve.—*See* Ratisbon.

Cologne.—1747–1755. *See* Liége.

1756–1780. Marked Cologne.

1781–1806. Marked Cologne and Cassel.

Note.—Two volumes belonging to this series are under Hesse Cassel.

Frankfort.—1665–1703. *See* Ratisbon.

1703–1709. Marked Frankfort.

Then follows another series.

1745–1750.

Hamburgh.—The regular series marked ' Hamburgh,' commences 1662 to 1780.

Then a new series from 1781 to 1807, about 121 volumes besides odd volumes and loose papers.

See also Vol. II. of the Hanover Correspondence; also Sir Leoline Jenkins' Collection, 1673–1683, page 59.

FOREIGN or DIPLOMATIC CORRESPONDENCE — *continued.*

German Princes and States — *continued.*

Hanover.—*Note.* Made the Ninth Electorate in 1692, and erected into a kingdom at the Congress of Vienna 1814.

One series 1689–1814. Then there is the Regency Correspondence separated from that of Hanover, 1719 to 1755. *See* 'Regency' under the Domestic arrangement.

There is another series marked 'Hanover, Brunswick, Hesse Cassel, 1775 to 1783.'

There is also another series from 1780 to 1810.

Hanse Towns.—*See* Hamburg and Germany.

See 'Trade Papers' under the Domestic arrangement.

Heidelburg (Palatinate)—There is a volume under this head, but it belongs to the head 'Hesse Cassel.'

Hesse Cassel.—Marked 'Cassel, 1716–1719.'

Cassel Heidelburg, 1719.

Note.—There is a volume of this series under 'Heidelburg.'

Cassel, 1727–1729.

Wolfenbuttel and Cassel, 1730–1731.

Note.—There are two volumes here which belong to the Cologne series.

Hesse Cassel, 1807–1810.

Liége.—1743 to 1755. Three volumes. Liége, Brussels, Cologne.

Maestricht.—1759–1763.

Manheim.—One volume, 1724–1726.

Munich.—1746–1759, about eight volumes. There is a volume under Ratisbon belonging to this series, marked 'Ratisbon and Munich.'

Ratisbon.—A volume marked 'Ratisbon, Cleve, Augsburg, Frankfort, 1665 to 1703.'

About 16 volumes, marked 'Ratisbon, 1702–1766.'

Saxony.—*Note.* The Elector of Saxony became King of Poland, 1697. Saxony elected into a Kingdom by Treaty of Cosen, 1806.

The volumes placed under this Head of 'German Princes — Saxony' belong to the Poland series. *See* Poland; Prussia, vols. 55, 56; and Saxony.

Wolfenbuttel. *See* Hesse Cassel, 1730–1731.

FOREIGN or DIPLOMATIC CORRESPONDENCE — *continued.*

GERMANY—Vienna.

>There are about 250 volumes of this Correspondence of the Empire commencing as early as Ed. II. 1311, but the Correspondence and Papers before Hen. VIII. are very inconsiderable.

>The first series is, as stated above, from 1311 to 1780; then commences a new series under the head Austria, 1781 to 1814. There is one volume marked 'Trieste, 1756–1806.'

>*See* also Sir Leoline Jenkins' Collection, 1674 to 1684, p. 59; also Stepney's Collection, pp. 55–58.

HAMBURG.—*See* 'German Princes—Hamburg.'

HANOVER.—*See* 'German Princes—Hanover.'

HANSE TOWNS.—*See* 'German Princes—Hanse Towns.'

HELIGOLAND.—1808–1810. Six volumes.

HOLLAND:—

>The following observations are intended to point out to those desirous of searching the Correspondence of the Low Countries the necessity of searching both that under the head 'Flanders' and that under the head 'Holland' together, during the time of the troubles which led to the separation of the United Provinces from the other parts of the Netherlands.

>It would seem to be difficult to draw the exact line when the Correspondence of the Netherlands should be separated into 'Flanders' and the 'United States' or 'Holland.' The Union of Utrecht, 1578–9, Jan. 29, has been considered as the foundation of the Republic of the United Provinces; but this does not appear to be the time to draw the line of separation of the Correspondence. In electing the Duke of Anjou for the head, the States merely withdrew their allegiance from one Sovereign and transferred it to another. At the death of Anjou, 10th June 1584—the assassination of the Prince of Orange, 10th July 1584—the renewal by the Confederates of the Act of Union of Utrecht on 14th July 1584—and indeed Zealand and Holland immediately choosing the second son of the Prince of Orange (Maurice) for their Stadtholder—all seem to combine to draw the line about 1584. After Anjou's death the Confederates entered into negotiations with France, where their Ambassadors were received in the

FOREIGN or DIPLOMATIC CORRESPONDENCE — *continued.*

Holland — *continued.*

> same form as the Ambassadors of other Powers; this Correspondence, therefore, might be considered as the Correspondence of the ' United Provinces ' or, as they have now become, ' Holland,' as separate from that of Flanders.
>
> There is a great mass of the early Correspondence which requires to be finally examined, arranged, and bound.
>
> Besides the above there are about 340 vols. 1678 to 1780
>
> Then commences a new series -   - 1781 to 1810
>
> There is also a series marked ' Rotterdam,' 1745 to 1780, about 44 volumes.
>
> *See* also Sir Leoline Jenkins' Collection, 1673 to 1684, p. 59; also Stepney's Collection, pp. 55, 56; also Williamson's Collection, pp. 77–79.

HOLSTEIN.—*See* ' Denmark.'

HUNGARY.—*See* ' Germany—Vienna '; also Stepney's Collection, pp. 55–58.

ICELAND.—One volume marked ' Iceland, Foreign and Domestic, Dec. 1809 to Dec. 1810.'

INTERCEPTED CORRESPONDENCE :—

> Geo. II. and III., being copies of letters of Foreign Ministers from and to England.

IONIAN ISLANDS.—1778–1809.   Eleven volumes.

> *See* also a volume under the head ' Malta,' marked ' Milan, Zante, Malta, 1686–1755.'

ITALY.—*See* ' Rome and Italian States '; also Sir Leoline Jenkins' Collection, 1675–1684, p. 55.

MALTA :—

> There is a vol. marked Milan, Zante, Malta, Chevaller Baltiulle, 1686–1757.
>
> "   "   Malta, Mr. Dodsworth, 1756–1763.
>
> "   "   "   Consuls Dodsworth and Rutter, 1764–1769.
>
> "   "   "   Consul England, Captain Ball, and Grand Master, April 1789 to Dec. 1800.
>
> "   "   "   Sir Alex. Ball and Mr. England and Grand Master, Jan. 1801 to Nov. 1806.

FOREIGN or DIPLOMATIC CORRESPONDENCE — *continued.*

MILAN.— *See* a volume under the head ' Malta '; also, ' Rome and Italian States.'

Various information will be found touching Milan in the French, German, and Spanish Correspondence.

Note.—The King of France was Master of the Milanese from 1500 to 1512, and again possessed it in 1515, and held it till 1521, when Sforza took possession as Duke of Milan, and remained so, subject to divers misfortunes and contentions with France and the Emperor until 24th Oct. 1535, when the Emperor Charles V. seized Milan as a fief of the Empire, and on the 11th Oct. 1540 invested his son Philip in the Duchy; this Prince, and all the Kings of Spain his successors, possessed the Milanese until 1706, when the Emperor Joseph made himself master of it, and Charles VI., his successor, confirmed himself in possession by Treaty of Buda, 1714.

MILITARY.—English Auxiliary Armies and Foreign Expeditions :—

Marlborough Correspondence - - }	18th May 1702 to Nov. 1711.
Duke of Ormond - - -	April to Nov. 1712.
Earl of Stair, &c. - - -	- 1742–1743.
Marshal Wade, &c. - - -	- 1744.
Duke of Cumberland, &c. -	- 1745–1748.
Colonel Amherst - - -	- 1756.
Colonel Durand - - -	- 1758–1760.
Commissary Boyd - -	- 1758–1760.
Duke of Marlborough -	- 1758–1760.
Marquis of Granby, &c. - -	- 1758–1763.
Prince Ferdinand of Brunswick -	- 1758–1763.
Colonel Clavering - -	- 1760–1763.
Hesse Cassel - - -	- 1756–1763.

MINISTERS. Foreign Ambassadors:—

There is a series of Papers marked Foreign Ambassadors, 13 volumes, 1710 to 1752, viz.—

Vol. I. Letter Book of the Secretary of State, containing Copies of Letters to the various Foreign Ambassadors resident in England, and Copies of Letters from the Foreign Ambassadors to the Secretary of State, &c., 1710–1713.

FOREIGN or DIPLOMATIC CORRESPONDENCE — *continued.*

Ministers — *continued.*

      Vol. II. Original Letters of Foreign Ambassadors, and Drafts of Letters to Foreign Ambassadors, 1731.

      III. to X. Similar, 1732–1741.

      XI. XII. Letter Books (Copies of Letters) to and from Foreign Ambassadors, 1741–1748.

      XIII. Original Letters from Foreign Ambassadors to the Secretary of State, and Draft Letters to them, 1744–1752.

    Note.—At the end of some or most of the Foreign Correspondence, that of the Foreign Minister will be found to have been kept distinct from that of the English Minister; and is probably similar to what in the more modern Foreign Correspondence is placed at the end of each volume as Domestic, being the Correspondence of the Foreign Ambassador with the Secretary of State, &c. in this country.

MOROCCO.—*See* ' Barbary States.'

NAPLES.—*See* ' Sicily and Naples.'

NICE.—*See* ' Savoy.'

NIMEGUEN :—
    An immense mass of Correspondence, &c. relating to the Treaty of Nimeguen. *See* also Sir Jos. Williamson's Collection, p. 79.

PERSIA, 1807–10. Four volumes.

POLAND, 1675–1796. 116 volumes. *See* also ' Saxony.'
    See also Stepney's Collection, pp. 55–58.

PORTUGAL :—
    The early Correspondence is not arranged.
    There are, however, 67 volumes of one series, besides six volumes marked ' Ministers,' and three volumes marked ' Consuls.'
    This series begins   -   -   - 1692–1782.
    Another series of 100 volumes   -   - 1781–1810.
    See also Sir Leoline Jenkins' Collection, 1642–1684, p. 59.

FOREIGN or DIPLOMATIC CORRESPONDENCE — *continued.*

PRUSSIA :—

For the earlier Correspondence, See 'German Princes—Brandenburg.'

See also Stepney's Collection, pp. 55–58 ; also Sir Leoline Jenkins' Collection, 1673–1682, p. 59.

There is a series commencing 1698–1780. 115 volumes.

Another series - - 1781–1810. 84 volumes.

Note.—The Elector of Brandenburg was proclaimed King 1701 ; he was confirmed in his dignity by Treaty of Utrecht.

ROME and ITALIAN States :—There is a mass of unarranged Papers ; also three volumes, 1518–1544.

ROYAL LETTERS :—

They are arranged according to Countries, chronologically.

First series, 30 volumes, Hen. VIII. to Anne. To which there is a Calendar.

Second series, 38 volumes, Anne to Geo. III. Ditto.

Note. —Royal Letters much earlier than Anne are to be found in this series, certainly as early as Eliz.

Third series, 26 volumes, from about Car. II. to 1780, to which there was a rough draft of a Calendar.

Fourth series, 17 volumes. Ditto.

There are also bundles of Royal Letters arranged chronologically in Countries.

The Scots Royal Letters are at present incorporated with the Scots Correspondence.

Note.—When the above Royal Letters were selected and arranged, there does not appear to have been any fixed rule as to what constituted a Royal Letter, or if there was, it was probably erroneous, hence much of what is now arranged under the head of 'Royal Letters' would more properly belong to the regular Correspondence of the country to which it relates. Different persons will take different views of this subject. But the principle now acted upon in the State Paper Office is, that a letter written from one Royal Person to another is a Royal Letter ; but all letters sent from the English Sovereign to his Ambassadors abroad belong to the Correspondence of the country to which it was sent, and is not kept separate as a Royal Letter. In like manner any letter sent from the Sovereign to any of his Representatives in England, Ireland, or the Colonies, is not considered a Royal Letter.

D

FOREIGN or DIPLOMATIC CORRESPONDENCE — *continued.*

RUSSIA :—
> The regular series commences 1673–1780.
> New series   -   -   -   1780–1810.

SAVOY and SARDINIA :—
> There are 3 volumes 1613–1620, and a mass in bundles.
> There is also a series from 1691–1810.
> *See* also Sir Leoline Jenkins' Collection, p. 59.

SAXONY :—
> The Elector became King by Treaty of Cosen, 1806.
> For the early Correspondence, *See* 'German Princes—
> Saxony, Poland.'
> The new series of Correspondence is from 1781 to 1806,
> 18 volumes.

SCOTLAND :—
> Although there are some few papers of early date, the
> Correspondence generally commences temp.Hen.VIII.:
> this series of Papers, therefore, thus stands as to
> date from 1290 to 1602; the Correspondence then,
> by reason of the accession of James to the throne of
> England, became *Domestic. See* Scotland, under the
> head 'Domestic.'

SECRETARIES' LETTER BOOKS (Foreign) :—
> There are about 100 volumes from about 1695–1775.

SICILY and NAPLES :—
> One series of 29 vols. 1, 2, 3, marked 'Naples,' 1684–1733.
> 4, 5,   „   'Messina,' 1689–1733.
> 6,   „   'Naples,' 1734–1755.
> 7,   „   'Messina,' 1734–1755.
> 8 to 29,   „   'Naples,' 1739–1779.
> A new series of 42 vols.   „   'Sicily,' 1780–1810.

SPAIN :—
> There are 9 or 10 volumes 1558–1620.
> There is a series from 1672–1810.
> There is also a mass of unarranged.
> *See* also Sir Leoline Jenkins' Collection, 1673–1684,
> p. 59.

SWEDEN :—
> There are three volumes   -   1630–1704.
> There is another series, 1689–1810.   185 volumes.
> *See* also Sir Leoline Jenkins' Collection, p. 59 ; also
> Stepney's Collection, pp. 55–58.

SWITZERLAND.—Berne, Geneva, &c.
> 67 volumes, from 1689 to 1799.

FOREIGN or DIPLOMATIC CORRESPONDENCE — *continued.*

TREATIES :—

Note.—The Prothonotary in Chancery was the officer who formerly made out and enrolled all Treaties, Leagues, Ratifications, Commissions, Orders, and Powers to Ambassadors, Envoys, &c., and other matters between the Sovereign of this country and Foreign Powers, and the Enrolments are in the custody of the Master of the Rolls, down to 22 Jac. I., since which time the Prothonotary ceased to bring them into the Rolls Chapel.

The duties of the Prothonotary ceased and became a sinecure long before the office was abolished, which took place by Stat. 2 & 3 Wm. IV. c. 111.

The original treaties in the State Paper Office are from about 1528 to 1762, to which there is a Calendar in two parts, forming four volumes; two volumes Geographical and two volumes Chronological; each country is designated by a particular letter, viz. Vol. I. of the Calendar Geographical, 1528–1712; Vol. II. 1713–1762.

A. Emperor of Germany.
B. France.
C. Spain.
D. The States-General.
E. Portugal.
F. Denmark.
G. Poland.
H. Sweden.
I. Prussia.
K. Savoy and Sardinia.
L. Russia. ⎱ No treaties with these during the
M. Modena. ⎰ period which the first volume of
N. Genoa. ⎰ Calendar embraces.
O. Rome.
P. Treaties of Marriage.
Q. Treaties with German Princes.
R. Treaties with Switzerland and the Hans Towns.
S. Tuscany. ⎱ No treaties with these
T. Empress Queen of Hun- ⎰ during the period
gary. ⎰ which the first vo-
U. Treaties with Eastern ⎰ lume of Calendar
Princes. ⎰ embraces.

FOREIGN or DIPLOMATIC CORRESPONDENCE — *continued.*

Treaties — *continued.*

 Attached to the second volume of Calendar is a Calendar of Treaties transmitted since the forming of the above Calendars.

 The two volumes of the Chronological Calendar contain, of course, the same matter as the above, under a different arrangement.

 There is also a great mass of Negotiations or Treaty Papers,—Cologne, Nimeguen, and Utrecht.

 See also Sir Joseph Williamson's Collection, pp. 76–81.

 Also Sir Leoline Jenkins' Collection, p. 59.

 Also Mr. Stepney's Collection, pp. 55–58.

TRIESTE.— *See* 'Austria.'

TRIPOLI.— *See* 'Barbary States.'

TUNIS.— *See* 'Barbary States.'

TURKEY :—

 The early Correspondence not arranged.

 One volume, 1604–11.

 A series, 1684–1810.   110 volumes.

 See also Stepney's Collection, p. 58.

TUSCANY, FLORENCE, and LEGHORN :—

 A series from 1684–1780.   Besides such as are not arranged.

UNITED PROVINCES.— *See* 'Holland.'

VENICE :—

 There is a Collection, Hen. VII. and VIII. and some unarranged.

 There are three volumes, 1612–1616.

 Also 38 volumes, 1689–1800.

WILLIAMSON, Sir Joseph. — *See* Separate Collections, pp. 60–83.

WIRTEMBERG :—

 The Duke became King, 1800, by Treaty of Presburg.

 There are three volumes of Correspondence, 1797–1807.

5. LIST OF CALENDARS AND INDEXES.

DOMESTIC:—

Domestic generally, a Calendar temp. Hen. VIII. and part of Ed. VI. One volume.

A Calendar of the Domestic of the time of Eliz. is forming.

A Calendar of the Domestic of the time of Jac. I. is formed in draft.

Borders.—*See* Scotland and Borders, next page.

Calais and Boulogne. Hen. VIII., Ed. VI., and Mary. One volume of Calendar.

Criminal Papers, 1687–1780. Two volumes. A Calendar.

Deeds, Leases, &c. Hen. III. to Car. II., and Certificates of Musters, Hen. VIII. to Car. I. A Calendar.

Gunpowder Treason Papers, Jac. I. A Calendar.

Indentures of War.—*See* Privy Seal.

Interregnum Papers. Index to Books of Orders of Council of State, 1648–9 to 1659. One volume.

Alphabetical, numerical, and County Indexes to second series of Composition Papers.

Indices Nominum et Locorum to first series of Composition Papers.

Ditto   ditto   second series.

Ireland. A Calendar, Hen. VIII., Ed. VI., and Mary. Two volumes.

Note.—There is also a mass of alphabetical memoranda, temp. Eliz., irregularly taken, chiefly with the view of assisting to assign dates to undated Papers.

Law Papers, 1684 to 1768. Calendar. One volume.

Local History. Calendar. Two volumes.

Petitions, Eliz. to Car. II. inclusive, Alphabetical Calendar. Two volumes.

Petitions and References, and Attorney and Solicitor General's Reports, 1660 to 1678. A particular Calendar of subjects attached to each volume.

Petitions and Reports and Orders in Council, Car. II. A Calendar at the end of each volume.

Privy Seal Writs and Warrants, and Indentures of War. A Calendar divided into parts,—Part 1. a brief Calendar of the nature of the Writs, 1216 to 1547: Part 2. Indentures of War, 1327 to 1509. The Preface to the Calendar contains an account of the various places in which the documents had been located.

CALENDARS AND INDEXES — *continued.*

Domestic — *continued.*

Signings by Stamp, by Hen. VIII.   Sept. 1545 to Jan.
1547.   There is an Index of Names of persons and
places contained in the documents signed by Stamp.

Sign Manuals.   7 Jac. I. (1609), to 18 Car. I. (1643).
One volume.   The Calendar to these documents was
formed while the documents were in bundles; they
are now bound in volumes.

Trade Papers, Fisheries, and Plantations, 1542 to 1761.
Three volumes.

Warrants or Dockets, 1661 to 1711.   Six volumes of
Index; also two volumes of General Index, 1660 to
1722.

Warrant Books of Scotland.   A Calendar at the end
of each volume.

There is also a Calendar to Papers relating to the
History of the State Paper Office.

COLONIES :—

East India Papers, 1581 to 1783.   One volume of Calendar.

FOREIGN or DIPLOMATIC :—

Flanders, Hen. VIII., Ed. VI., and Mary.   Two volumes
of Calendars.

France, Hen. VIII., Ed. VI.   Two volumes of Calendars.

Germany, Hen. VIII., Ed. VI., and Mary.   Two
volumes of Calendars.

Rome, Venetian, and Italian States, Hen. VIII.   1 volume.

Royal Letters, Hen. VIII. to Anne.   Six volumes.

Scotland and the Borders, Hen. VIII.   One volume.

Treaties ; Calendars, Geographical and Chronological.

Flanders, France, Germany, Italy, Spanish, Swiss.
There are Calendars to each.   These are the Papers
brought from the Chapter House.

There is also an Alphabetical Index of British Ministers
resident at Foreign Courts, Car. II. to 6 Geo. III.
One folio volume, compiled by Mr. Rich. Ansell.

There is also an Alphabetical Index of British Ministers
abroad, Hen. VIII. to about Geo. II., compiled by
Mr. Lechmere, the Deputy Keeper of State Papers.

There is also a volume marked 'Diplomatic Index and
Notes—Ambassadors,' noting the time when Ambassadors went and returned—formed by Sir Jos. Williamson.

6. SEPARATE COLLECTIONS.

(1.) CHAPTER HOUSE PAPERS.

There were a great many volumes removed from the Chapter House to the State Paper Office in 1832, of the reign of Henry VIII., which have not been incorporated with the rest of the State Papers, viz. —

Cardinal Wolsey's Correspondence.
Cromwell's ditto.
Sir Thos. Wriothesley's ditto. One volume.
Lord Lisle's ditto, while Lord Deputy of Calais; this series of Papers also contains Lord Lisle's private or domestic correspondence with his wife, &c.
Miscellaneous letters to the King and Council.
Also a volume of Foreign, &c.

(2.) COLLECTION OF MR. GEORGE STEPNEY.

Note.—There is a large collection of Stepney's Papers in the British Museum, to which there is a MS. Catalogue in the Reading Room.

The following is a brief list of Mr. Stepney's Correspondence and Collection of Papers, from about 1689, at the State Paper Office; this is about the beginning of the Correspondence, though some of the Papers collected are much earlier, but the earlier Papers seem to be in volumes of Miscellaneous Papers.

A volume marked 'Treaties, 1689–1695.' The first part is, the Grand Alliance, 1689. In 1692, Powers for Sir H. Colt to treat with the Dukes of Brunswick and Lunenburg, towards bringing them into the Grand Alliance, and other Papers relating thereto. Sir H. Colt's Credentials and Instructions as Envoy Extraordinary to Saxony.

Sir H. Colt died in the beginning of Sept. 1693, whereupon Mr. Stepney received orders to quit Vienna, where he had been employed as agent for 10 months, and to repair to Saxony to carry on the negotiation which Sir H. Colt had begun. *See* p. 74 of this volume, and p. 75 is Mr. Stepney's Instructions; and following is his Correspondence; and at p. 129 commences a summary of his negotiation; p. 148, his Credentials as Minister to the Landgrave

SEPARATE COLLECTIONS (*Mr. G. Stepney*) — *continued.*

of Hesse Cassel, $\frac{30 \text{ Oct.}}{9 \text{ Nov.}}$ 1694. He was also at the Hague; *see* p. 149 the treaty he made with Baron Goertz. In January 1694–5 he received fresh Instructions as Minister to the Elector of Saxony and Landgrave of Hesse Cassel: this will be found further on in the Book (no page).

Vol. marked 'Hague, &c.' 1690–2. This seems to be Sir H. Colt's Copy or Entry Book.

Vol. marked 'Berlin, &c.' 1692.

Vol. marked 'Vienna, Dresden, &c.' 1693, 1694. An Entry Book.

Vol. marked 'Dresden, 1694.' Copies and Entries.

Vol. marked 'The Association of the Six Circles,' 1696, 1697. Copies.

Vol. marked 'Poland and Sweden.' A Collection of Papers relating to Poland and Sweden, 1696, 1697. Death of King of Poland, 1696. Death of King of Sweden, 1697. Contents at the beginning.

Vol. marked 'Berlin, 1698.' It contains Mr. (George) Stepney's appointment as Ambassador Extraordinary to Brandenburg, 1697–8. Instructions. Credentials. Ceremony observed. Correspondence. Entries and Copies of Letters. A Contents at the beginning.

Vol. marked 'Berlin, 1698–9.' This contains Copies and Entries of his Correspondence, 1699. Contents at the beginning.

Vol. marked 'Berlin, 1699.' Similar to the above.

Vienna and Hungary.

Vol. 1. marked 'Vienna, from 1 April to June, 1701.' Mr. Stepney's Instructions, appointed Envoy Extraordinary to Vienna, 9th March, 1700–1. Credentials. Journey. Observations on different matters on his route. His interview with different Princes. It will be seen, by a letter from Mr. Secretary Hedges to Mr. Stepney, that he also received letters of credence to the Electors Palatine, Cologne, Mentz, and Treves, and Bishop of Würzburg, dated 1st April 1701. His arrival at Vienna. Correspondence. These are copies. There is an Index at the end.

SEPARATE COLLECTIONS (*Mr. G. Stepney*) — *continued.*

Vol. 2. (Copies) marked 'Vienna, tome 2, July to Sept. 1701.' There is an Index at the end.

Vol. 3. (Copies) marked 'Vienna, tome 3, Sept. to Dec. 1701.' A Contents at the beginning and end.

Vol. 4. Missing.

Vol. 5. (Copies) marked 'Vienna, tome 5, March to Aug. 1702.' No Index.

Vol. 6. (Copies) marked 'Vienna, tome 6, Sept. to Dec. 1702.' No Index.

Vol. 7. (Copies) marked 'Vienna, tome 7, Jan. to March, 1703.' An Index at the end.

Vol. 8. (Copies) marked 'Vienna, tome 8, April to June, 1703.' Index or Contents at the end.

Vol. 9. (Copies) marked 'Vienna, tome 9, July to Sept. 1703.' No Index.

Vol. 10. (Copies) marked 'Vienna, tome 10, Oct. to Dec. 1703.' No Index.

Vol. 11. (Copies) marked 'Vienna, tome 11, Jan. to March, 1704.' It will be seen by reference, 26th Jan. 1703-4, in this volume, that Stepney was to have Credentials to treat with the Elector of Bavaria. Hungarian matters will also be found in this and the following volumes. There is no Index.

Vol. 12. (Copies). The back of this book is torn off, but it should be marked 'Vienna, tome 12, April to June, 1704.' There is a Contents at the end.

Vol. 13. (Copies) marked 'Vienna, tome 13, July to Sept. 1704.' Contents at the end.

Vol. 14. (Copies) marked 'Vienna, tome 14, Oct. to Dec. 1704.' Contents at the end.

Vol. 15. (Copies) marked 'Vienna, tome 15, Jan. to June, 1705.' No Index.

Vol. 16. (Copies) marked 'Vienna, tome 16, July to Dec. 1705.' No Index.

Vol. 17. (Copies) marked 'Vienna, tome 17, Jan. to June, 1706.' No Index.

SEPARATE COLLECTIONS (*Mr. G. Stepney*) — *continued.*

Then follow three volumes concerning the Hungarian Mal-
contents, viz.—

> Vol. 1. (Some Copies and some Originals) marked
> 'Hungary.' A Collection of Papers relating chiefly
> to Hungary. Mr Stepney's Letters, &c., 1704, 1705.
> A Contents at the beginning.
>
> Vol. 2. (Copies and Originals) marked 'Hungary.'
> Journal of the Negotiation between the Malcontents
> and Vienna. Letters, &c., 1705, 1706.
>
> Vol. 3. (Copies and Originals) marked 'Hungary, 1706.'
> Continuation of the Negotiation.

Miscellaneous.

> Vol. marked 'Papers in German,' of divers dates, 1614,
> 1636, 1657, 1692, 1686, &c. It is a book of Copies.
>
> Vol. The first Paper is a Copy of the Treaty of Oliva,
> 3d May 1660; after which is a collection of Papers
> relating to Poland and Sweden, 1701 to 1705, of
> which there is a Contents.
>
> Vol. marked '1705, 1706.' This is chiefly about the
> Lordship of Mundelheim (Mindelheim): Correspon-
> dence of Marlborough with Stepney, wherein Marl-
> borough leaves Stepney, as it is expressed, *to settle it.*
>
> There is a volume put here as Stepney's, marked 'Berlin,
> 1680.' This seems to be the entry book of Sir
> Robert Southwell, 1680; his Credentials and In-
> structions to Brandenbourg are prefixed to this volume.
>
> Another volume marked outside 'Papers in German;' a
> miscellaneous volume of Papers in German, Latin,
> French, English, and some Poems. A Contents at
> the beginning.
>
> Another miscellaneous volume. The first Paper is the
> Treaty of Westphalia, between Sweden and Belgium,
> 1681. The next, a Letter from Cardinal Mazarin;
> Letters of the Queen of Sweden, 1650; Regulation
> for Trade and Navigation of the French Isles and
> Colonies in America, &c.
>
> Another, marked 'Adrianople, Constantinople.' It
> seems to be an early entry book, touching the affairs
> of Turkey, Lord Paget's Correspondence, &c.; relation
> of his voyage from Vienna to Adrianople, his au-
> dience, &c. There is a Contents at the beginning.

SEPARATE COLLECTIONS — *continued.*

(3.) COLLECTION OF SIR LEOLINE JENKINS, Secretary of State to Charles II.

Note.—This Collection is in course of incorporation with the regular Foreign Correspondence.

	Number of Volumes.	Date.
Barbary States	1	1680–1684*
Brandenburgh	1	1673–1682
Courland and Holstein	1	1645–1682
Denmark and Sweden...................	3	1673–1683
Flanders	4	1674–1684*
France	6	1669–1684
Germany	8	1674–1684
Hamburg....................................	1	1673–1688
Holland......................................	5	1673–1684
Italy	3	1675–1684
Portugal...............	1	1642–1684
Sardinia	1	1676–1684
Spain	2	1673–1684
Tangiers	3	1671–1684
Negotiations at Nimeguen	1	1676–1678
Ditto, Letters from Sir J. Williamson	1	1675–1677
Domestic	21	1660–1684–5

* Incorporated.

The last five volumes consist of four volumes of Petitions, and one volume of detached Papers relating to the Duke of Monmouth, Lord Russell, Earl of Essex, Algernon Sydney, &c. 1683, 1684.

SEPARATE COLLECTIONS — *continued.*

(4.) COLLECTION OF SIR JOSEPH WILLIAMSON.

Sir Joseph Williamson was appointed Keeper of State Papers on the last day of 1661, which office he held until his death in 1702; in 1673–1674 he was Ambassador to treat of Peace at Cologne; and in 1674 he also became Secretary of State. He formed a Collection of Papers, &c., and bequeathed them to the State Paper Office.

His Collections at the State Paper Office are at present separated into two different portions, and kept distinct from each other in different parts of the office, viz. —

Collection I., of which the *First Series* consists of 40 volumes, under the following heads :—Treaties, Ratifications, Instructions, Commissions, Declarations of War, Ambassadors, Consuls, Admiralty, Navy, Military, Lieutenancy, Ordnance, Musters, Oaths and Obligations, Treaties of Marriage, Declarations and Proclamations, Discoveries, East and West Indies: of this series there are also five large volumes, four of which are General Treaty Books, and the fifth volume contains Miscellanies and Instructions.

Second Series, 19 volumes, viz.—Copies and Extracts of Treaties, 1558 to 1669; Miscellaneous, 1509 to 1698; Treaties of Marriage, 1293 to 1667; Declarations and Proclamations, 1541 to 1698; Commissions and Patents, 1573 to 1641; Original Commissions, Miscellaneous, 1545 to 1638. Also a Diplomatic Index and Notes of Ambassadors. It contains Notes of the time when Ambassadors were sent to and returned from Foreign parts, and other Diplomatic Notes.

Note.—The Foreign part of the above Collection is in course of incorporation with the regular Foreign Correspondence.

Collection II. For greater convenience of reference this Miscellaneous Collection has been placed under the respective heads of Domestic; Law; Miscellaneous; Pamphlets; Books relating to the History, Constitution, Revenue, Nobility, &c., of different Countries; Alphabetical Books, or Book for the alphabetical arrangement of the matters they contain; Ireland; Plantations and Foreign Dominions; Records; Diplomatic and matter pertaining thereto; Treaties; Styles and Titles; Precedency; Ceremonies.

SEPARATE COLLECTIONS (*Sir J. Williamson*) — *continued.*

The following brief Calendar, however, will afford a better idea of this Collection.

Note.—These Books generally bear two numberings. The Nos. in the first column indicate an old numbering. The Nos. in the second column show the order in which they stand with respect to the different heads, Domestic, Law, &c.

Domestic.

267	1	A true copy of the Roll of the Proceeding in an Appeal of Treason before the Constable and Marshal, between Thomas Lord Morley, Appellant, and John de Montague Earl of Salisbury, Defendant; anno primo Henrici quarti.
61	2	Five Books tied together, being Informations in June 1683, touching the taking away the lives of the King and Duke of York, intended Insurrections, &c. There is an Alphabetical Index, &c.
36	3	Marked ' Valuations of Livings.' On the first leaf is written 'Joseph Williamson, copied for me by Dr. Lamplugh, at Oxford 1667–8.' Then follows a Table of the various Counties, number of Benefices, and annual value; after which, a Table of the names of the Benefices in the different Counties, and their annual value.
37	4	Valuations of Livings. This is similar to the above; but this has at the end of each County the names of the Religious Houses, distinguishing whether Priories, Monasteries, Hospitals, Nunneries, &c.
—	5	A Table of the Parishes of the City of London.
306	6	List of Pensioners on the Chest at Chatham.
—	7	Marked ' Trade—Council of Trade.' Proceedings of Council of Trade, at Mercers' Hall, London, 1660.
78	8	Rules for granting Passes for Ships and Vessels.
141	9	Entries of Passes.

SEPARATE COLLECTIONS (*Sir J. Williamson*)—*continued.*

281   10   Marked 'Fees due to the King's Servants, &c., upon Creations, Appointments.'

237   11   Notes by Sir Jos. Williamson, Chronological, respecting Parliaments, when and where held — Proceedings in Grants of Charters — Subsidies, Benevolences, &c.—commencing Hen. I. to Charles I. Names of Chancellors and Speakers.

—   12   Articles of War.

173   13   Charter of Merchant Adventurers.

Law.

46   14   Speculum Juris Publici Anglicani, or a Mirror for an English Minister of State, wherein may be viewed the Resolutions of several Queries jurisprudentially given by the learned and grave sages of this realm, relating to His Majesty's Prerogative both in Ecclesiastical and Temporal affairs; to his Consort; to the Prince; to His Majesty's Grants, Pardons, Forests, Customs, Counties Palatine, Seals, Proclamations, Commissions, Corporations, Monies, Courts; together with other matters not improper for the cognizance of a Minister of State.

57   15   Speculum Juris Politici, or a Mirror for a Grand Minister, touching Government; collected out of History and other Books 1673; Ship Money; Hampden's Case. An Index at the end.

285   16   Speculum Juris Publici; Mirror for an English Minister; Resolutions, &c. concerning Aliens, Ambassadors, Leagues, Jurisdiction, Parliament, High Court of King's Prerogatives, &c.

55   17   Marked —'Manuscript—Law Miscell.' — Court of Chancery, Abuses, &c., Declaration concerning the Title of Prince Charles to Duchy of Cornwall, Letter of King Charles touching borrowing money, and divers law points.

SEPARATE COLLECTIONS (*Sir J. Williamson*) — *continued.*

56   18   Marked—' Manuscript—Law **Miscell.**'—King's Prerogative. Collection relating to Allegiance, Union **and Separation** of England and Scotland, **Conquests,** Prerogative in Gold and Silver, **Coining,** Bulwarks, Distresses, Reservations, Exemptions, Swanerds, Penal Statutes, Letters Patent, False Rumours, Fairs, Markets, Toll, Idiots, &c. (Presentations to Benefices, 367.)

60   19   Collection of Rules and Orders relating to **the** Court of Chancery.

—   20   Relating to the High Court of **Justice.** A small book, 12mo.

252   21   Concerning **divers Law Matters.**

65   22   Notes on **divers Law Cases.**

59   23   Dissertation on Public Law.

—   24   **Marked** ' Law of Nations,'—Points, Libels, &c. Illustrated by Extracts of Letters, &c.

—   25   Marked ' Law of Nations,'—Navigation, Commerce, &c.

Miscellaneous.

—   26   Marked ' Domestic Miscellanea.' There is a Table of Contents.

39   27   Divers Foreign Pedigrees. An Index at the end.

75   28   Questions propounded and agreed upon to be sent to Teneriffe; a brief experimental account of the production of some colours. Divers experiments to be made, &c.

182   29   Poem (Acrostic) addressed to the Plenipotentiaries of the King of Great Britain.

296   30   Divers forms of Instruments, mostly in Scotch.

312   31   A Book in Dutch, on Fortification.

96   32   Posts; when they set out — when they arrive; Foreign and Ireland; at the beginning and end of the Book.

    1663. — Notes from News-Letters; Domestic and other Notes; Lieutenants, and principal persons in each county.

SEPARATE COLLECTIONS (*Sir J. Williamson*) — *continued.*

— 33 Marked 'Collection of Letters, Speeches, &c.;
          Walter Raleigh, &c.' Contains:—

Le Pardon de Madame la Comtesse de Somer-
    set, 1616.

Speech of Ellesmere, Chancellor of England,
    when he was made principal Justice of
    England.

Sir Henry Montague's Speech when sworn
    Lord Chief Justice, 1616.

La Harangue de Monsieur de Vair, when he
    was déposé de l'état du garde des Sceaux,
    1616.

Answer of King James to the Inhabitants of
    Cambridge, when they required their town
    to be made a city, 1616.

Chancellor Ellesmere's Petition to quit his
    Office, 1616.

Letter to Sir Edward Coke when Chief Justice
    of England, 1616.

Sir Walter Raleigh — Letter to his wife,
    Nov. 1618.

Ditto, Verse made the day before he was
    sentenced.

Ditto, his Account of his Voyage to Guinea.

Ditto, his Letter to the King, Oct. 1618.

Ditto, his Apology (p. 54); his Death (p. 57).

Field, the Player, to Mr. Sutton, Preacher at
    St. Mary Overs, 1616.

An Apology for Earl of Essex, 21 pages.

Sir Thomas Egerton's (Lord Keeper) Letter to
    Essex; his last words; and last words of
    Cuff, Secretary to Essex.

Speech of Sir Francis Bacon on taking his
    place in Chancery.

Speech of Bishop of Lincoln when made
    Keeper of the Great Seal.

Submission of Sir Henry Yelverton, Star
    Chamber, 27th Oct. 1620. His Speech,
    1621 (p. 93).

Letter of Thomas Allured against Prince
    Charles marrying the Infanta.

SEPARATE COLLECTIONS (*Sir J. Williamson*) — *continued.*

231   34   Records, &c.—Parliament Rolls; Inquisitions; Patent Rolls; Abstract of Privileges granted to Merchants of the Staple; Divers Transcripts; Letter of Archduke Ernest, 1595; the Lady Elizabeth's answer, made at Hatfield, 26th April 1558, to Sir Thomas Pope, sent by the Queen's Grace to understand how she liked of the marriage motion made her by the King Elect of Switzerland's messenger; Henry Cuff, Secretary to Essex, his letter to Secretary Cecil declaring the effect of the Instructions by the Earl of Essex, and delivered to the Ambassador of the King of Scotland, touching his title to the Crown of England; Ledington's letter, (Secretary of Scotland,) 1566, touching title of Queen of Scots to the Crown of England; directions of Queen Mary, touching the Reformation of the Church; Letter of Queen Elizabeth to King of Scots, 1601, touching increase of pension, &c.

85   35   Marked inside ' Randolph, 1629,' contains:—

The Office and Power of the High Treasurer and Surintendants des Finances of France.

King of Spain's revenue—from whence it arises.

A Declaration of the Office of High Treasurer of Scotland.

A true Collection as well of all the King's Offices and Fees of any of the Courts of Westminster as of all the Offices and Fees of His Majesty's Household; all fees appertaining to Captains and Soldiers having charge of Castles, &c. in England; Offices and Fees of his Highness' Houses, Parks, Fortresses, and Chaces.

Declaration of the Revenue of the Pope—how raised.

Declaration of the Revenue of Florence—how raised.

Abstract of Treaty of Marriage between Queen Mary and Philip of Spain.

E

SEPARATE COLLECTIONS (*Sir J. Williamson*) — *continued.*

>Abstract of Treaty of Marriage between Arthur of England and Catherine of Castile, 1496.
>
>Abstract of Treaty of Marriage between Henry and Catherine of Castile, 1503.
>
>Points of Treaty between Hen. VIII. and Francis of France, for marriage of his daughter with the Dauphin, 1518.
>
>Abstract of Treaty of Marriage between Hen. VII. and Margaret Duchess of Sebaude, Sister to Maximilian the Emperor.
>
>Abstract of Treaty of Marriage between James King of Scots and Margaret daughter of Hen. VII.
>
>Contract of Marriage between the Lady Elizabeth and Frederick Elector Palatine, 1612.
>
>Juramentum Consilarii; Oaths of the Secretary of State; of the Master of Requests; of the Clerk, Keeper, and Register (Thomas Wilson) of His Majesty's Papers and Records for matters of State, p. 153.
>
>Ceremonies observed at the Coronation of the Empress of Hungary. An Index at the end.

70   36   Notes, Scraps, Advertisements. A large volume. The following is written by Sir J. Williamson: 'The authorities and quotations inserted in this collection are taken out of the underwritten Authors in their several subjects, and to them the pages cited are to refer; Parliament Rushworth's Collection, Part I. II., &c.; Rushworth's Collections; King James's Works; My book of Miscellaneous Collections in 4to., according to their vols. 1, 2, 3, &c.; Strada, History of the Low Countries; Davela; Grimstone's History of Spain; Ricaults' Turkish History; Spottiswood's Hist. Scotland; P. Paoli's Hist. Council of Trent.'

232   37   Divers Notes, under alphabetical arrangements, with reference to his own (Sir J. Williamson's) MSS. Collection.

SEPARATE COLLECTIONS (*Sir J. Williamson*) — *continued.*

234 38 Notes of Grants and Commissions, &c.; Creations under alphabetical arrangement, giving the date of the reign. Very curious.

The following · are two or three heads at random :—

Farthings.—11th July, 2 Car. I., Grant to the Duchess of Richmond of the sole making of Farthings.

Robes.—Under this head will be found the Appointments to the Office of Keeper, &c.

Trade.—Commission granted to inquire into divers matters. Licence to import, &c.

Voyages.—Commission to Sir W. Raleigh, concerning his voyage into the south part of America, 13 Jac. I.

180 39 A very large bound book. Notes arranged under alphabetical heads, Treaties, Diplomatic, &c. An Index at the beginning.

Names of Ambassadors who negotiated the Treaties, Agreements, &c.

— 39 a Names of Strangers residing in London.

— 39 b Passes.

304 40 Note Book, too various and confused to describe.

143 41 A large volume of notes.

68 42 Marked ' Day Book.' It is in Sir J. Williamson's handwriting, being his notes respecting Foreign Countries, Names of Foreign Officers, (Ministers, &c.) and divers notes.

298 43 Memorandums, or Day Book, 1670–1673.

97 44 1678. Diary. Sir J. Williamson's handwriting.

138 45 The following is written on the first leaf :—" A Collection of some parte of the French L^rs which I wrote in the time of my service at Court, under Sir F. Walsingham, Knt., Her Majesty's Principal Secretary; some for Her Majesty; some for Earl of Leicester, my master; and to some of my private friends. Lisle C. D. E." The letters are from 1571 to 1588, all in French.

297 45a Against the changing of Arms of Families.

SEPARATE COLLECTIONS (*Sir J. Williamson*) — *continued.*

— 46 Letters, Lord Cranbourne; Lord Treasurer, &c.
1604–1611, on various subjects.

— 46*a* A Note Book.

— 46*b* Scrap Book, marked 'Gazette.'

Pamphlets.

67 47 Pamphlet called 'Tom Tell Truth, or a Discourse of Rumours of the Times;' also the answer. 'The Practice of Princes, and Lamentations of the Kirk,' written by Lord Baltimore, late Secretary of State.

27 48 Pamphlet, being a dispute between a Councillor of State and a Justice of Peace, touching the calling of a Parliament.

79 49 Pamphlet (in Italian), entitled 'The Speaking Animals,' in which the different Princes in and out of Europe are represented speaking.

    Aquile   Imperatore
    Gallo   Francia
    Volpi   Spayna
    Pardi   Inghelterra, &c.

— 50 Pamphlet called 'Political Arithmetic.'

Books relating to the History, Constitution, Revenue, Nobility, &c. of different Countries.

274 51 A Treatise of the Succession of the right heirs to the Crown of England in remainder.

275 52 A Treatise of the Nobility, according to the laws of England. How they are known. Liberties by Charter. Description of the word 'Nobilitas.' Contention between competitors for honour. Laws of Chivalry. Creation, &c. A Table of Contents at the beginning.

151 53 The State of England, 1600, by Thomas Wilson. Point of Succession, King James, A. Stuart, &c. Pedigree of Kings of England from the Conqueror. Number of Kingdoms. Qualities of the Countries, &c.

167 54 The State of England since the uniting of Wales.

149 55 Secret History (in Italian) of all the Princes of Italy, 1665.

SEPARATE COLLECTIONS (*Sir J. Williamson*) — *continued.*

162	56	Description of the Principalities of Italy (in Italian).
152	57	Marked 'Italy Collections,' Engravings of Cardinals, Popes, &c.
—	57 *a*	A volume marked 'Papel Ymport de Ytalia.'
163	58	Marked inside, 'Italy, &c., Collections, 1667, &c., J. W.' Engraved Portraits of divers Italian Archbishops, Nobles, Officers, &c., and divers matters relating to Italy.
169	59	An account of the Court of Rome by the Venetian Ambassador (in Italian).
42	60	Marked 'Relaĉon of Principal Families of Rome' (in Italian). There is an Index at the end.
229	61	Discourse upon the Republic of Genoa (in Italian).
164	62	Marked inside by Sir. J. Williamson, 'Notitia Hispaniarum; the State of Spain, 1668, copied out of a piece communicated to me by Mr. Godolphin, 1667.—J. W.'
165	63	Marked 'Campanella.' An account of the Monarchy of Spain by Thomas Campanella (in Italian).
171	64	State of Sweden, its Constitution, Revenue, &c. List of Nobility.
157	65	Marked 'Cities and States.' On the first page is written the following:

'Ambrose Randolph. My father, Mr. Thomas Randolph, was sent Ambassador to Scotland, 1564, 1569, 1585, 1586, 1587. Was sent to France, 1573, about the marriage with Monsieur, 1574, 1576. He was sent also into Muscovy, and Germany, and the Low Countries.'

The book is mostly written in Italian, describing divers countries, their affairs, &c. At page 38 will be found the last Instruction of Philip. II. of Spain to his son, written in English. At the end of these Instructions is written the following :— 'Thus much hath bin saved out of those bills and writings which were sent to be burnte.'

SEPARATE COLLECTIONS (*Sir J. Williamson*) — *continued.*

168   66   On the first leaf is written, ' States of Countryes —Italy.' Describes the proceedings of foreign countries; sometimes by way of Journals, sometimes by the Ambassadors, &c. Letters and extracts, temp. Eliz., pp. 263, 267, are dated, 1599, 1600; p. 291 is a survey of the State of the Great Dukes of Tuscany, 1596; p. 453 is dated 1599; p. 479 is dated 1592; p. 643 is an account of the Fees paid to several Officers of the Republic of Venice; the Revenue; Charge and extent of that Republic; p. 1093 is an engraved plan of the Conclave, the procession with the Pope's body, his lying in state, election of the new Pope, &c.

—   67   Marked ' State of Countries.' France, Spain, Portugal, Revenue, Household, Offices, &c., shown by extracts of Ambassadors' and other letters, &c. There is a Contents at the end.

—   68   Marked ' State of Countries.' Germany, Turkey.

—   68 *a*   Discourse on Genoa.

Alphabet Books.

50   69   Alphabetical Index to four volumes of Books of Minutes. Charles II.

236   70   Alphabetical Book :—Notes.

238   71   Alphabetical Book : — Notes, marked inside by Sir Joseph Williamson, ' Sweden, Denmark, Poland, Russia, Turkey, 1673–4, and 78, collected in those years.—J. W.'

242   72   Alphabet Book.

243   73   Alphabet Book.

245   74   Alphabet Book.

246   75   Alphabet Book:—Notes, Diplomatic, England, Ireland, &c.

250   76   Alphabet Book:— Names of Scotch Nobility, their families and arms described. Same of the English.

251   77   Alphabet Book.

254   78   Alphabet Book:—Divers matters.

SEPARATE COLLECTIONS (*Sir J. Williamson*)—*continued.*

255 79 Alphabet Book :—Names of persons in England, what they are, their religion, politics, &c. Notes, or a kind of Spy Book.

240 80 Alphabet Book :— Names of divers places in Germany, to whom they belong, names of persons, who they are, &c.

239 81 Alphabet Book : — Names of foreign persons, who they were, &c.

247 82 Alphabet Book : — Names of foreign persons, who they are, their offices, &c.

248 83 Alphabet Book :— Notes by Sir J. Williamson tied to 248, &c.

291 84 Alphabet Book : — With references to books which do not appear. The references are, however, alphabetical.

— 84 a Alphabet Book.

— 85 Marked 'Preachers— Congregational and Anabaptist,'—County Alphabetical Index, being a list of persons and places where Presbyterian, Congregational, and Anabaptist Preachings are.

58 86 A Catalogue of all the books entered in the Register Book of the Company of Stationers, from 26th March 1676 to 2d Nov. 1677.

59 87 Catalogue of Books.

83 88 Sir Joseph Williamson has written on the first leaf the following :—' This is a collection containing the heads or arguments of the MS. Books of Collections of Sir Julius Cæsar, as they remained in the hands of his Grandchild, 1676.' (It is beautifully written.)

— 89 A bundle of Letters, Instructions, Petitions, &c.

Ireland.

58 90 Notes relating to Ireland—Chronological. The first part of the book is a list of Officers of Ireland, arranged chronologically ; to this part there is an Index.

SEPARATE COLLECTIONS (*Sir J. Williamson*) — *continued.*

69   91   Scrap Book, relating to Ireland, arranged under heads, for instance :—
       Parliament in General.
       House of Commons' Powers.
       Chief Governors.
       Lord Chancellors.
       Popery, &c. &c.

253   92   Alphabetical Index, relating to Ireland.

—   93   Relating to Ireland ; Principal Families and Chiefs, their Pedigrees, Laws, Customs. An Index at the beginning of the book.

       Scotland. The latter part of the book relates to Scotland ; Pedigrees of Chief Families, and divers notes ; to which there is an Index.

Plantations—Foreign Dominions.

63   94   Marked inside by Sir Jos. Williamson, ' Plantations, For. Dominions.'
       A small Book of Notes, by Sir Jos. Williamson.

Records.

202   95   Perambulations of the Forest, made 29 Ed. I.

—   96   Transcript of the Liber Rubeus Scaccarii.

9   97   Lands holden *in capite.*

—   98   Francia Rolls, being a Collection of 143 French Rolls remaining in the Tower of London.

      98 *a*   Francia Rolls.

—   99   Rotuli Franciæ, ab 16 Ed. III. ad 21 Ed. IV.

—   100   Ditto ditto, ending 22 Ed. IV.—Treaties and Truces. Also, Notes of divers Grants, &c., relating to Vasconia. This book is not bound.

—   101   Rotuli Vasconiæ.

—   101 *a*   Extracts.

—   102   A small bundle marked ' Cinque Ports.'

—   103   Extracts.

227   104   Inquisitions *post mortem.*

SEPARATE COLLECTIONS (*Sir J. Williamson*) — *continued.*

212	105	Escheats and Inquisitions, Ed. I.; written on vellum.
213	106	Similar to 105, but later period.
214	107	Extracts from Records, Grants of Lands, &c.
215	108	Extracts from Domesday Book, arranged alphabetically.
216	109	Extracts, probably Inquisitions.
192	110	Inquisitions, Escheats, temp. Hen. III. or Salop.
193	111	Inquisitions, Grants of Lands. Index of Persons at the end.
195	112	Ditto. An Index.
199	113	Ditto, Extracts from Pat. Rolls, Ed. I. to Rich. II.
200	114	Ditto.
201	115	Ditto.
188	116	Ditto.
208	117	Ditto, County Cambridge.
209	118	Ditto, divers Counties.
257	119	Ditto, Pat. Roll, Hen. III.
295	120	Marked ' Norfolk.'
—	121	Pat. Rolls.
—	122	Pat. Rolls, Hen. VIII.
219	123	Extracts from Parl. Rolls.
—	124	Charter Rolls; Charters granted to divers places. A very thick volume.
300	125	Marked outside ' Merchants of the Staple 1670,' and several other transactions of great value.
		At the end of this volume are divers loose papers of Sir Jos. Williamson's Notes respecting a Queen Heiress, her Husband, &c., as well England as other countries. Notes from a Treatise on Monarchy, Power of the King, &c.
233	126	Marked ' Miscellanea.' A Collection of Records in the Tower, of all Houses, Castles, Lands, Services, Advowsons, Knights' Fees, and other Possessions which the Earl of Arundel died possessed of.

SEPARATE COLLECTIONS (*Sir J. Williamson*) — *continued.*

273 127 Commissioners of Array, Martial Law, Raising Subsidies, &c.

211 128 A brief Collection of all Forests, Parks, Chaces, Woods, &c. in England, extracted from Records in the Tower of London, beginning John, and ending Ed. VI.; dated 1654–5.

203 129 Marked ' Creations.'

261 130 Grants, &c.

268 131 Grants of Castles, Forts, Sea Ports, Towns, &c., Ed. I.

205 132 Royal Letters, taken ex Rot. Clausarum, Ed. I. to Hen. IV. A Calendar at the beginning.

210 133 Certain Grants, &c. of Offices and Lands, Officers of State.

An Account of the Rolls that are placed in the hole in the Study.

Appointments of Officers of State, &c.

Constables of England, Sub-Constables. First Appointment 46 Ed. III.

Clerk of the Hanaper, 33 Hen. VI.

Serjeant-at-Arms, 16 Rich. II. to 22 Hen. VI.

Chancellor, 16 Hen. III. &c., and other Officers in Chancery.

Protector Duke of Bedford, Hen. V. & VI.

Gangell, Ed. II.

Treasurer of the Household (Thesaurar. Hospicii Regis), 9 Ed. III. to 34 Hen. VI. under this head.

Treasurer of England, &c.

Comptroller of the Works, &c. (Contrarotulator opačonū aut clicus opačonū).

Harp-player to Queen Margaret (Citherator Reginæ), 37 Hen. VI.

Steward of the Household (Senescall Hospicii), and his Officers, Ed. IV. to Hen. VI.

Clerk of the Market (Clicus Mercati).

Shoemaker.

Apothecary.

Falconer, &c. &c.

SEPARATE COLLECTIONS (*Sir J. Williamson*) — *continued.*

Spigurnelli in Chancery. ⎫ *See* also for this office
Notary. ⎭ under 'Chancellor.'

Officium Vibriatrie.

Household.
  Pavilion, Confessor, Promptaurius, Pannus,
    Coronator.

Assayer and Comptroller of the Money.
  Cambriator, Cementarius.

Officium Cementar.
  Mason, Galeator, Vitriarius, Carpenter, &c.

Officium vocat Oterhunt.

Secretary to the Queen, 20 Rich. II.

Marshal of England, 1175, &c.

Wardrobe-keeper.

Clerk of the Crown.

Treasurer of the Chamber (Thesaur. Cameræ),
  27 to 37 Hen. VI.

Constable of England, Edw. III. to Hen. VI.

Magne Elemosinar. (Grand Almoner), Hen. IV.
  to Hen. VI.

Admiral of England, Edw. III. to Hen. VI.

Equisium Regis, Edw. III.

Pincerna Angl. Edw. II. to Hen. VI.

Chancellor of the Exchequer, Edw. II. to
  Hen. VI.

King's Bench, Attorneys, &c., Attorney
  Generals and other Officers.

Custodia Rotulorum in Banco, the different
  Officers.

Ditto, in Chancery.

Ditto, Privy Seal, Hen. III. to Hen. V.

Camerar. Scaccarij, Edw. III.

Remembrancer of the Exchequer, Edw. II. to
  Hen. VI.

Alnager, Edw. I. to Hen. VI.

Palace of Westminster, Officium Privati Palacij
  Regis Westm., Hen. VI.

Master of the Dogs (Officium custodiendi
  Canes), Hen. VI.

SEPARATE COLLECTIONS (*Sir J. Williamson*) — *continued.*

> Swanherd, Edw. III. to Hen. VI.
> Clerk of the Parliament, Edw. IV. to Hen. VI.
> Officium faciendi Loricas (q. Armourer).
> De Castris custodiend., Edw. III. to Hen. VI.
> Surgicus Regis.
> Officium Garbellatoris omnium speciarum, Hen. VI.
> Justiciar., Edw. III. to Hen. V.
> Cambium auri et argenti, Hen. III. to Hen. VI.
> Moneta et Monetarii, John to Hen. IV.
> Water Bailiff (Custodia Aquarum).
>
> > There are a few leaves at the end of the book so badly written that they are scarcely to be made out.

288	134	
290	135	
319	136	
249	137	
235	138	
224	139	
217	140	Extracts from Records.
223	141	
222	142	
220	143	
221	144	
218	144a	

Diplomatic, and Matters pertaining thereto.

— 145 Marked ' France.—Negotiations from 1544 to 1677;' Notes of Negotiations; Ambassadors, their Instructions, &c.; there is an Index.

139 146 Marked ' France.'—Two Notes respecting Calais, 1556, 1557; Names of English and Foreign Ambassadors in France; English Governors of Havre-de-Grace, &c.; Names of French Officers of State.

Separate Collections (*Sir J. Williamson*) — *continued.*

— 146 a Marked ' Carey's Relation of France.'

— 146 b Marked ' Hist. France.'

— 146 c Marked ' France and Spain.'

93 147 Holland.—Interregnum; Negotiations of the Deputies of the States General of the United Provinces of the Low Countries sent into England in order to a treaty between the two nations, 1653.

101 148 Marked inside ' War with Holland, &c., 1671–2.' Letters of the Earl of Arlington—Seizure of Dutch Ships; Sir W. Lockhart's Instructions, &c.; Letters to the Duke of York, Lieutenant-Admiral; Additional Instructions to the Duke of Richmond going Ambassador to Copenhagen; Articles for joining English and French Fleets; Articles for regulating Statutes; Treaty between Cologne and France; Striking to English Admiral; Instructions to Duke of Bucks and Earl of Arlington going Ambassadors Extraordinary to French King; Treaty of Heeswick; Commissioners to the Lords of Foreign Committee jointly with French Ambassador, to treat with Portugal on what grounds that State may enter war against the States; Instructions for Prince Rupert going to sea as Admiral and General; Instructions and Commission to the Earl of Sunderland, Sir Leoline Jenkins, and Sir J. Williamson, Plenipotentiaries at Cologne.

102 149 Marked inside ' Holland 1672, Duke of Bucks, Earl of Arlington, &c., Embassy and Negotiation'— Powers of the Plenipotentiaries; Powers to Duke of Monmouth; Commission to Sir Jos. Williamson to be Secretary to the Embassy; their letters, &c.

104 150 Marked ' Negotiations D. M. ye warre with Holland, 1672–3–4. Assembly at Cologne, S. W.'

SEPARATE COLLECTIONS (*Sir J. Williamson*) — *continued.*

105 151 Marked inside by Sir J. Williamson, 'England and Holland.—The Two East India Companies; Copyes of Papers put into my hands and otherwise layd by me together in order to the Treaty at Cologne, 1673.—J. W.'

106 152 Marked by Sir J. Williamson, 'Journal 1673–4.' The book, however, commences 1671–2.

107 153 Marked by Sir J. Williamson, 'Diary 1673–4, at Cologne.'

108 154 Marked inside by Sir J. Williamson, 'Cologne Dispatches, *i. e.* Ambassadors to Lord Arlington; Lord Arlington to the Ambassadors.'

     N.B. This entry book was made and kept by the Secretary of the Embassy, Mr. Chudleigh, by order of the Ambassadors.

109 155 Marked inside by Sir J. Williamson, 'Cologne.—My Journal Book, 1673–4; from Jan. 1673–4 to May 1674.—J. W.'

110 156 Copies touching Treaty of Peace at Cologne; Instructions for Sir Leoline Jenkins and Sir J. Williamson going Ambassadors, dated May 1673; Earl of Arlington's letters to them; Revocation of Sir Leoline Jenkins and Sir J. Williamson, dated 27th March 1674. Articles of Treaty of Peace towards the latter end of the book.

111 157 The same subject as No. 110.—Their Passport; Form of their Commission to treat jointly with the French Plenipotentiaries; divers letters of Sir J. Williamson, and matters touching their negotiation.

112 158 Same as 110 and 111. Also a List of Papers sent relating to the matters of the Flag and Fishing. *See* also the end of this Calendar.

113 159 Cologne.—Passage of Sir Leoline Jenkins and Sir Jos. Williamson, their arrival, letters, &c.

SEPARATE COLLECTIONS (*Sir J. Williamson*) — *continued.*

114 160 Copies of Correspondence of Sir Leoline Jenkins, Sir J. Williamson, and Earl of Arlington, 1673, 1674, from Cologne and the Hague.

115 161 Marked 'Cologne.' Same as 114. Also Letters addressed by the Mediators to the Dutch Ambassadors; and Correspondence with the Dutch and Spanish Ambassadors. Table of Contents at the beginning.

116 162 Marked 'Cologne.' Journal of Proceedings from June to January, 1673–4.

     162 *a* Abstract of Mr. Chudleigh's Entry Book of Cologne Despatches, 1673, 1674.

117 163 A Journal or Narrative of the Proceedings between the Commissioners appointed by His Majesty and the Commissioners deputed by the States-General, pursuant to a Treaty of Peace made at Westminster, Feb. 1673–4, concerning a Treaty Marine to be observed throughout the world. Also an Article particularly relating to the English and Dutch East India Companies, concluded 1674.

134 164 Mediation Journal, 1675–6.

135 165 Marked inside 'Journal. Various Notes by Sir J. Williamson, 1676, 1677.'

     166 ⎫
     to ⎬ Nimeguen Negotiations.
     168 ⎭

140 169 Marked 'Ryswick Journal.' Journal of Proceedings at Ryswick, June to August 1697.

316 170 A Bundle respecting Holland.

 98 171 Marked inside by Sir J. Williamson, 1667–68, &c. 'The Triple alliance and ye severall peaces relat^t to it. J. W.' There is a Table of Contents.

 99 172 Marked 'Foreign Committee, from Nov. 2, 1667 to 22 June, 1679.' The notes are in Sir J. Williamson's writing.

SEPARATE COLLECTIONS (*Sir J. Williamson*) — *continued.*

100   173   Foreign Committee?   Written inside by Sir
            J. Williamson, 'Journal—Minute Book—War
            with Holland 1671-2.'   The last date is in
            1673.

            There are others than that which should
            belong to the Foreign Committee.   Are they
            the Notes of Proceedings of the Privy Council?
            The King was generally present.

118   174   Foreign Committee?   Sir J. Williamson's Notes
            as to divers places, matters, and things, from
            1674 to 1679.   There is an Index at the end.

119   175   Foreign Committee Book.   Notes of matters and
            proceedings, 1675–6 to 1677.

136   176   Foreign Committee Book from 20th Aug. 1676
            to 25th Aug. 1678.

159   177   Marked on the back 'Holland—Flanders.'   This
            contains names of Ambassadors, Commis-
            sioners, Agents, Governors, &c., in Holland
            and Flanders, from temp. Hen. VIII.

103   178   Alphabet Book, marked inside by Sir J. William-
            son, 'Holland, 1673–4 and 78.'   Names of
            Officers, Ambassadors, &c.   Names of Places.

160   179   Marked 'England.'   Names of early English
            Writers and their Works; Appointments of
            Officers of State; names of English Ambas-
            sadors abroad; Foreign Ambassadors in
            England; matters concerning the Univer-
            sities; and divers curious and useful notes
            from temp. Hen. VIII.

13   180   Marked 'Catalans.'   Extracts of Letters; Lex-
            ington's Instructions to Madrid; his Corre-
            spondence, &c. 1712 to 1714.   At the end of
            the volume is some earlier Correspondence and
            Instructions respecting the Catalans and Spain
            generally.

            Instructions to Mitford Crow, 1705, 1706;
                Ditto   to Earl of Peterborough, to Sir
            Cloudesley Shovel, 1705, 1706, &c.

SEPARATE COLLECTIONS (*Sir J. Williamson*) — *continued.*

170 181 Marked 'Spain.' The commencement of this book is an Index to divers genealogies at the other end of the book; then follow the names of English and Foreign Ambassadors at different periods, Foreign Governors, Viceroys, Foreign Officers of State, Diplomatic Notes, &c. Eliz., Jac. I., Car. I., Commonwealth. At the other end of the book, inside the covers, is marked 'N.B. The Notes here taken are out of Grimstone's Hist. of Spain. Lond. 1612.' Then follows a Catalogue of persons that have been Ambassadors, Agents, &c. in Spain. After which divers Pedigrees relating to Spain, the Index to which is at the other end of the book.

158 182 Marked 'Italy, Switzerland, Savoy.' Names of English and Foreign Ambassadors. Various Diplomatic Notes, Eliz. to Car. I.

161 183 Marked 'Germany—Poland.' Names of English and Foreign Ambassadors, Officers, &c.

      183 *a* Diplomatic (Volume).
      183 *b* Ditto   (Bundle).
      183 *c* Ditto   (Ditto).

Treaties.

72 184 The first entry is 'The most Weighty, Secret, and last Instructions given by Philip II. of Spain to his Son.'
      Treaty with Spain, 1630; King of Spain's Oath, for the observance of it.
      Ditto concerning Palatinate Wars.
      Ditto of Marriage of Chas. I. and Henrietta. .
      Ditto with France for Restitution, 1631.
      Ditto   ditto   of Commerce, 1632.
      Articles of Treaty between English and Dutch, touching the Indies.
      Cessation of Arms in the East Indies between Spain and England, 1635, upon the Peace of 1630. And many other Treaties.

175 185 Marked 'Treaties' made by King Chas. II.

      185 *a* Index of Treaties.

F

SEPARATE COLLECTIONS (*Sir J. Williamson*) — *continued.*

Styles, Titles, Precedency, Ceremonies, &c.

SEPARATE COLLECTIONS (*Sir J. Williamson*) — *continued.*

28   187   Styles, Titles, &c.   The following note is in Sir
J. Williamson's writing, ' Procured for me by
the means of Monsr Richards at Paris, about
1675 or 1676.'   The title of the book is,
' Souscriptions, Soubscriptions, Inscriptions.'
Styles and manner of addressing different Sove-
reigns.   Example :—
Au Pape.

   Souscription - Tres Sainct Pere.
   Soubscription - V͂te devot fils de Roy de
          France et de Navarre.
   Inscription - A Notre tres St. Pere le
          Pape.

188
to   } Styles, Titles, &c.
205

Printed by EYRE and SPOTTISWOODE,
Her Majesty's Printers.

www.ingramcontent.com/pod-product-compliance
Lightning Source LLC
La Vergne TN
LVHW012201040326
832903LV00003B/57